Adventures of a Bougie New Yorker

a clever and satirical romp through the Orange County California School System

---

Stephanie Neal

Copyright © 2021 Stephanie Neal
All rights reserved
First Edition

Fulton Books
Meadville, PA

Published by Fulton Books 2021

This is a work of fiction, and any resemblance to a real person or persons is entirely coincidental.

ISBN 979-8-88731-473-0 (paperback)
ISBN 979-8-88731-474-7 (digital)

Printed in the United States of America

Acknowledgement

It's truly remarkable how some people leave a lasting imprint on our hearts, and there's one person in particular who has had an enduring impact on me.

Alexandra, your honesty and integrity have consistently guided and inspired me, even when it meant facing uncomfortable truths. Your unwavering support has been a constant source of strength, and for that, I am deeply grateful.

Shannon, my dear sister, I want to express my heartfelt appreciation for embodying grace and dignity in every aspect of your life. Your strength and resilience in the face of challenging circumstances have been a continual inspiration to me. While you are Dr. Keenan in class, you continue to educate and motivate me at home, and for that, I am truly thankful.

Mom, the infectious laughter you provided, encouraged me to pursue this book further. Thank you for all the happy memories. I love you.

To my husband, Jeff Neal, I want to extend my gratitude for your unwavering kindness, patience, and countless late nights that turned into early mornings as you listened to me read and reread these pages. Your unwavering support and belief in me throughout the two years it took to complete this book have meant the world to me. Your selflessness, kindness, and boundless love are qualities that I cherish deeply. I love you, Dr. Neal.

STEPHANIE NEAL

Pops, thank you from the bottom of my heart for being the embodiment of strength and courage throughout the years. We all have been blessed to have you in our lives. I love you.

> Miracles do happen
> You must believe this
> No matter what else you believe about life,
> You must believe in miracles
> —Augusten Burroughs

Introduction

And the excitement builds; my outfit is perfect, my hair—just right, and my makeup not too much. My Porsche has been waxed. I am ready to make my first impression. My entrance, if you will. Yes, here I am—armed with sophistication and the scent of fresh ink on my diploma in early childhood education. Think of the countless young minds I will mold and shape, the lives I will touch. Onward and upward young souls, it's Ivy League or bust. First prep schools and onto the ivory towers of higher education.

I saunter in. Confident in my achievements, I announce my presence, "Hello, my name is Penelope, Penny for short."

"Really, that's wonderful," I say to the woman taking my paperwork. She has just informed me that once my background check is complete, human resources will take note of my previous salary, and I will be bumped up immediately. Wow, what a relief. Part-time (perfect). A raise within a week (perfectly perfect). Graduating cum laude in ECE will pay off, I think to myself. I will start as a student supervisor and let the higher-ups know I want to be a teacher just because I should. I mean, why not? I leave human resources with a smile, knowing I am on my way. I am directed to my first post near the lunch area, where I am promptly handed a fecking broom, a hideous neon orange vest (just like the people who commit felonious crimes picking up trash on the highway), and a piece of paper. Reality to follow.

Most people may find this amusing; however, I found this to be disgraceful and shockingly unacceptable. Flashback, Penny, I think.

What do I remember? I applied to the online application on *Indeed*, which read:

> Educators needed immediately
> Elementary school, Orange County
> Student supervisors needed 17.5 hours a week
> Kindergarten through fifth grades
> To assist in the daily supervision of students from kindergarten to grade 5

I remembered that the position appeared to be the perfect number of hours to resume my schooling. As I see it, a beginning on the path God has chosen for me. Many have been called—few have been selected. Never mind that, Penny, the role that I read and was explained to me over the phone. Hmm, I never did have a face-to-face interview with anyone now, did I? *I just want to type in here that I wanted a Facetime interview so that the_interviewers would see how aesthetically pleasing I am.* They insisted they didn't need to see me. I damn well beg to differ. Idiots. Well, I take umbrage. Orange County is all about aesthetics and physicalities. Where were these farm animals from bum fuck Oklahoma or Nebraska with birthrights to an agricultural industry? If they were to think back, was their most fun-filled night cow tipping?

The piece of paper that was given to me was the job description:

> Newport School District Elementary school student supervisor knowledge of:

- Elementary school children's behavior and characteristics
- Acceptable methods used in controlling students in lunch recess situations
- Ability to learn and enforce school rules
- Works firmly, tactfully, and effectively with students and the public

- Understand oral and written instructions
- Work cooperatively with others
- Reports unsafe conditions
- Uses positive reinforcement strategies and other appropriate techniques to assist students in the development of proper behavior and an appreciation of human diversity
- Ensures no authorized persons are on school grounds during recess and that students do not leave the grounds without permission.

Minimum qualifications:

- Elementary school children's behavior and characteristics
- Works firmly, tactfully, and effectively with students and the public
- Twelve-grade education or higher

I walk into Newport Elementary and immediately feel a chill that the entire office is wearing invisible right-winged masks. I can see through almost everything; some say I was born with a unique sense; I call it common. This feeling makes me uneasy because union and red commonly do not mesh. Staff, do not push your political bullshit on me. This is my first day. Jays us cripes.

I have issues with people over all. They try to make me choose a side. Just their look is asking me, "Hi, welcome aboard. Do you drive a Prius or a Range Rover?"

I fashion myself as an independent. Well, until 2020, I did. What a shit show. I often wonder what happened to our country after 9-11, and would it be too damn much to ask people to act as we did on 9-12? Yes, that is right, on 9-12. People think we haven't had World War III yet. That it is coming. We are in it right now, this minute, standing in it this nanosecond in time. Are you awake? Did you hand in your copies of "If I Ran a Zoo"? Did you get the jab? Well, why not! Get up off your knees and sing the goddamn national anthem!

Meet the team

I see our principal, Doc John Robert. I noticed his tailored mask and form-fit wrinkle-free clothing. You must know that Doc Robert disguises himself as a lefty by riding his Vespa to and from school. But someone told me he secretly hides a 2020 Ford Super Duty LWB Crew Cab at home—the largest truck built in America.

All the ladies from the PTA joined the PTA just to have a look at ole Doc Robert. He is the "cat's meow," as they used to say. It's a night out for the ladies and an excellent excuse to get all "dolled up" in their most exemplary fashion. Top-down, hair in the breeze, driving their upscale convertible Lamborghini Evo Spyders. One of the most expensive convertibles in 2020. Come to think about it. I think that's why our school has so much money. We get so many donations. I don't worry about ole Doc Roberts. He doesn't appear to have a roving eye. But maybe that's because his wife is a barbie doll. Perhaps he told her what he wanted, and they went to the same plastic surgeon that all of Orange County went to and turned her into the Stepford wife. You can have everything done today, from your toes to your a*hem, to your butt, and even to your growth hormones. And then you see that one commercial, "But what about that sagging neck you've always been worried about?" And the *Stepfords* quickly jot down that number.

And what's more? They all have the same cookie-cutter nose. (I don't mean the pig noses that the ladies wore in the '90s. They've come a long way since then.) But it's a lovely nose, just the same. But that's the problem; it's all the same.

I don't care what procedure you've had done to yourself. There is one thing for sure, ain't no fixing fuggly. Either you have the canvas already to begin with, or you're just shite out of luck. There is no in-between.

I can say that the employees were quite snobby toward me the first few days. Two ladies were at the food tables, one in the field and two posted by the swings and tetherball court.

But I really paid attention to how at least five brooms and pans lined up along the cafeteria wall, just waiting for a rubber glove to come up and grab it. Grab it by the handle and push that sucker right into that pan.

While I was instructed to observe the ranks the first few days, I couldn't help but notice these ladies needed help. They worked hard and were short-staffed. Even though they were bitches, I decided to pick up a broom and sweep. I certainly didn't like standing around, looking all pretty while these ladies were worker bees. Building up a sweat, standing in the heat, wearing sun hats, and walking with umbrellas while wiping their foreheads.

This was what was needed to break the ice. I now had gotten to know the team, and I'd be working 17.5 hours a week with them.

First off, let me introduce you to the super sweeper, Dorothy. Dorothy is a long name. So for the sake of my breath and typing skills, I will now refer to her as Dot. Dot loves Jesus. Dot gets annoyed when I tell her that he was approximately four feet tall when he was alive. She usually storms away muttering, heathen, or something of that nature. I do it on purpose.

To tell you the truth, Dot is probably the most unusual woman I have ever met. I mean that in the best way possible. For instance, Dot never tried a cigarette or marijuana. She dated her boyfriend, now her husband, and stayed a virgin until their wedding night. Come to think about it, that is why he married her in the first place. I have always been a skeptic, but hell, if you came from the family of origin that I did, you too would believe in the "too good to be true" theory. It is like the day you found out there was no Santa Claus. Once I heard that, I instantly looked up scholarly reports on the matter. Who was St. Nicholas? news.campbell.edu, and here, these nerdies at that school, who wear their three-inch black circle-rimmed glasses, are writing about an old man who lived two hundred years ago and was benevolent with three bags of gold. Do they have any idea what they just did? They humanized him. I never felt that Christmas "spirit" again. Ole Saint Nick was the spirit, and that spirit was taken from me a long time ago.

There are other things about Dot that make her unique too. For instance, her family escaped communist Romania when she was a child. The Soviet Union had expanded its borders to the west and now included most of eastern Europe. Although her memory is unclear about what happened, she listens to the stories passed down through the generations. Dot takes great pride in her heritage as a Romanian immigrant but even greater pride that her family arrived here as refugees and legally pursued citizenship as an American. She is an American patriot. Her family believed in the American dream and pursued that dream through hard work and dedication—but, overall, their belief in Jesus. They did not seek handouts from the government. They had no sense of entitlement. Instead, they were given only an opportunity, and they made the most of it so that their children would not wear the yoke of socialism or communism. For this reason, her senses are keenly attuned to decipher any socialist agenda hidden among a sea of words masquerading as government *aid*. She is terrified of what she sees on the news now in this country and worldwide. More and more *leaders* pursue a path toward a socialistic takeover and dictatorship of the masses. Inflation, gas and food price hikes, and empty shelves at the grocery store. What's even scarier is mandating children to get the vaccine so they can attend public school, yet watching teens drop dead on the playing field due to myocarditis.

A friend taped Dot speaking to the school board and sent it to me. She expounded on the horrors of communism and why her family risked escaping to live in the *free world*. She doesn't want her children to get the vaccine and should not be forced into it. There was more to her story, but I couldn't make it out because Dot was crying so hard it was barely audible. I'm proud of Dot. It takes a lot of courage to go up against authority.

Dot also has two bachelor's degrees. She holds Bible study women's groups at her home and serves natural teas and homemade scones at these gatherings. I like black tea and tarts. "Tonight, ladies, we will spend the rest of our lives studying the book of Matthew." I am cringing. It is not that I do not love Jesus; it is just that I do not have to go singing it like some looney tune that needs to develop another language because this one is a 2,000-year-old religion in English. Maybe she should be more progressive and teach it in Espanola, considering the number of immigrants coming through our southern border who make California their home. Perhaps you can give some lessons in English, Ms. Benevolence! How about you give it a try, kaaay? Because I know for one thing, you can ask anyone who lives in this Country where they would love to live if they could, and the two states that come up first are: California and then Hawaii.

Dot is the best mom, though. I mean it. She will run you over in the street if she must pick her kids up. I've been told after mistakenly asking Dot for a ride to work and was a minute late walking to the car, "I don't do late." If she "doesn't do late," that could only mean that she will drive up and smash your body right into the blacktop, where you become unrecognizable, just so she is not late. She has a six-thousand-pound Mercedes SUV, and I believe she could and would do it.

Here's another thing about Dot. No matter what I say, she thinks it's funny. I could be in a badass mood and make one gesture, and Dot will dry heave laughing. What is that called? I'm just curious if it has a name. When Dot gets snippy, I know to look at her lip. Above her lip, a little white pimple lingers. And so I take note. If I happen to speak to her on the phone and she's snippin' on me, I must ask her if she has a pimple on her lip. She stops what she is doing, pauses, and begins to laugh. Yup. That's Dotty. And she's an absolute neat freak. You could eat off her floors, and she's quite a chef to boot. You know those people who can't just make a tuna sandwich. They must add the dill, mustard, romaine, and colorful cocktail tomatoes and garnish them with more beautiful colors to balance the hues. Oy vey. Gimmee some rye toast and a pickle, and I'm happy. Plus, it takes me way too long to put things like that together. Timing is the hardest thing in cooking. I would have to start the evening before what takes Dotty a couple of hours. There are worse things in life, I guess. I do a damn good job on my makeup.

We also have Cher, who works the sweeper like nobody I've seen in the elementary school or the junior high school, which is located across the street from us. These girls aren't half as good-looking as us, yet they get paid more and don't have to sweep. Don't ask me; I want to know as well. They purposely antagonize us too. On their break, they run around the field, performing their exercises while we watch, wondering how they get the time and/or energy to do it. For feck's sake, it's no wonder they never have any openings on that side. It is like they graduated from the sweeper school. I bet they don't even have any ECE credits! What a bunch of douzies.

For six months, Cher had me convinced she was born in Wuhan. But it dumbfounded me why she didn't carry an accent if China was her mainland.

It wasn't amusing when I considered all the Wuhanian's commies. She even had two baby commies too. I wondered if the husband was a commie who stayed home and messed with our climate.

To tell you the truth, I've seen some weird stuff happening lately. First off, Texas is paying some tremendous debt for insulting the Chinese. They had snow and ice for a week. No heat, and food rations were running low. Coincidence? I'm afraid not. And recently, I saw some odd lightning and thunder. For example, an electricity matrix in the sky. I'll tell you I lived in many places, but this was man-made. I'd even tell fake news channels about it. Even if the public doesn't believe me, I'd be in a suitable arena anyway.

Cher played Switzerland all the time. You couldn't get her to speak about anyone in management or the team. Let's face it, someone's got to talk with a group of women. She minded her business and kept the sweep on. Never stopped for a minute unless she was arrested and probably wouldn't then because she was of the mindset she would disappear. Jaysus lady, you're getting paid $14 an hour. Take your fifteen-minute break, dammit. You're making us look bad. And do you know, nobody in management pushed us to take that break? I told those girls to take their break and that they were entitled. But nope, Cher was not having it. Sweep, sweep, into the wonky dustpan, into the garbage for Purply (introduction to follow).

Cher was beautiful too. I mean inherently. Shining long brunette hair and brown eyes. She kept her figure nicely (because of the gawd damn sweeping). I had to stay as far from her as possible, even if it meant going out into the field.

Deanna, the assistant principal, often wondered what I was doing out there, but I couldn't tell her there was a commie among us that just may bring more. I wasn't sure even Jesus could take these mutts on. Deanna was a God-loving woman too. She was soft-spoken and didn't let much rattle her cage. She was happily married and the most understanding woman I had met in a long time. Everyone felt they could go into Deanna's office, take deep breaths, and count to ten. Deanna's office was our sanctuary, and we never took advantage of her or the psyche wardroom she provided. I often wished she supplied us with two hots and a cot. Now that would be extremely impressive.

Even Funnel was no help. Her birth name is Cindy, but Funnel is a better-suited name. Some mornings, she needed rides to work. Usually, she sends pictures of dead people and dogs over her texting device at night. I suppose she feels close enough to you to talk about the people who have transitioned before her. In that case, she will even show you pictures so she can elicit the same sadness in you. It is like DWI (dialing while intoxicated) for those who haven't figured this out. But why me? I think you may know now why I call her Funnel. Funnel rarely makes a whole week of work. We expect that. It is not like I haven't been privy to people like this in my own world; I know the behavior and the excuses. Funnel is the only one I know of that needed a week off because the second vaccination shot did her in; now here comes a new booster. "Extra, extra read all about it," a new variant of COVID-19 infections rising in California as Delta gains ground! Sigh, another two weeks without Funnel. I will get more into Funnel later. Right now, I have an emergency. A student pooed in the sink. BRB.

I am back. We are reasonably certain we know who the perpetrator is. We caught him on video walking out of the gender-neutral bathroom. I give him a pass. He is only in fifth grade. I think they should have put him in special needs but overlooked him because he's not tall. I'm not kidding; this kid is three feet tall, if I were to guess. He's like a goddamn pygmy. People say I'm tall, but how they say it makes me feel like I'm Abe Lincoln. It's really weird.

This boy is leaving in a few months to go to middle school. They will potty train him there. I am not worried. *And do you know what? I had an editor who looked over my draft, and she took the poop part out. I said, "Why did you take the poop part out?"*

She said, "Because it's not believable."

I said, "But it happened! It stays in! Poop in!"

To put it mildly, I'm supposed to live in a universe that makes sense. Most of it does until I close the door behind me, and it's 10:00 a.m. The sun is shining brightly, but I can still make out Doris, ole Purple Paws, rummaging through the garbage to retrieve whatever edibles are left to give to the grandkids. Both have now caught on to the "save the edibles" game. I know this because I heard one-fifth grader say, "Hey, there's hobo." I turned my head to the left so hard that I got that burning in my neck. You know that burning that you can't move your neck for a bit because you want it to stop burning, but you moved it because you wanted to see something so shocking that you couldn't wait for your neck to catch up with your eyes? It was that kind of burn. There I see Purple's grandson in the third trash can. I know he's been through the previous two. I tell the student I don't want to hear that out of his mouth again. Still the truth is that the grandson does it continually throughout the day, even when we leave trays of food for him just so he doesn't have to do that. Don't ask me; I hear he's getting help from the school shrink. I wonder if this illness has a name.

I rub my eyes and say, "By George, it's happening again." I find I must think to myself about these hidden funnies. I've gotten in trouble before with what amateurs diagnosed as a "sick sense of humor." Perhaps it's their perverse way of deciphering it that makes them sick. Who cares? Let's get back to Purple Paws. I call her Purple Paws because her hands are crimped into a paw shape. It's like she's thrown too many baseballs in her day, but that's not possible because I'm sure she's suffering from COPD. I could tell by her breathing, and Dot said her car stank like cancer stix. I think the cancer stix makes the blood stop flowing at the fingertips, and they turn purple. I'm not an MD; for cripes sake, I'm just trying to tell you how the paws can get purple. You don't see that, except for the zoo. The animals can't leave and bring prepackaged food home, so theirs is not as good quality and is used like ole Purply. Purply is way past retirement age, but she also has job security. Try to rid yourself of a woman of that age who belongs to a union. Good luck! So she does what she can with what she has.

I haven't introduced you to Paula. Because Paula has tripolar personality disorders, I would be remiss and rude or misleading should I forget to mention just one of them. I'll start with the kickstart. The kickstart is the morning mood. This is when you don't know where you stand. Until Paula is there to give you a giddy good morning "sista" or breezy "whew" right by you. The wind chill factor can drop to 45° F on a 70° F morning. You don't have to have done anything offensive for this to happen.

Then there's the "oh no, she's in with the assistant principal again," and you just told her a very personal thing. Shit, shit, shit. How many times has Dot told you not to trust *Jezebel*?

Here we have Inez, the interloper. No matter whom I am speaking with, when, where, and what time of day, Inez will appear and interrupt my conversation. She will steer the person I am talking to in her direction and disregard me entirely. This is where it is fair sport to bring tackles and blocks into play to regain your possession. There are no rules, regulations, or penalties when Inez interferes with the game.

Now Perilous Paula needs all the attention. She will go to great lengths to get it. If you don't understand what I am saying, please reread the introduction to Paula paragraph before this. You may be a little slow on the uptake.

I've realized not everybody is cum laude, and I've made room for that adjustment in my writing. I've seen Paula jump on the lunch tables with a bull horn loud enough to pop a child's eardrum to ensure everyone could hear her and, more importantly, watch her. She could have easily been heard on the floor. But this one day, she wore a miniskirt that even I was embarrassed to look at. And as rumor would have it, the schools will start teaching sex education from kindergarten through to the third grade. Well, this is a mighty fine place to start, I thought. After all, they've just received a complete visual of the female anatomy.

Paula would often take me by the hand, introduce me to almost every child, and tell me what their mother drives and their type of "vavoom" figure, what their husbands do for a living, and how many siblings are in the family. Is this normal behavior, I ask you? Do you honestly think I give a rat's arse who these kids are and what their mother drives? Oh, but I forgot, this is OC. I'm supposed to care. Just gimme a broom. I want out of this uncomfortable situation! I was planning to teach. Do you understand, little boy and girl? I'm not here to envy the life of some other. And where is that increase?

Did I mention we wipe down tables too? There is this mad mixture of corona-killing viricide. This stuff is a crazy biohazard level 68. We should be wearing hazmat suits, or in a pinch, you could use them to clean a wound or highlight your hair. This invention has many uses. And Lord Fauci has not a thing to do with it. This complex and potent chemical compound is often referred to as hydrogen peroxide, which is a safe-mouth rinse.

Now, I'm asking my readers, would you hire a babysitter and expect them to clean your house? Wouldn't you think at least something would suffer? Multitasking with a child is not a good idea. A child could choke to death while you are picking up a pickle from the kitchen floor while they are playing with their goddamn Ms. Piggy's mobile in the crib. How about sudden infant death syndrome (SIDS) or crib death? Still an unexplained death, even with an autopsy. Honestly, the probability of this happening in an elementary school, with three women sweeping, is the chance that something will go unnoticed.

In contrast, the last pile of goldfish was grounded into the floor. It is being swept up and left behind by some rat-bastid kid who decided to give us something to do since we aren't doing enough for our meager wages. And I'm sure he has figured out I haven't spent enough on my $300 boots and $275 jeans. I need this job badly enough that I must put up with their bull crap. *Ding, ding, ding*, wrong!

"Hey, you, get over here right now! Are these your goldfish on the floor?" (Make sure you never give them time to answer.) "Pick them up. I'll hand you the broom. Do you do this at home? Then why would you do this here? Next time I see you do this, you will be sent to Doc Robert's office. He has a nice cozy chair just waiting for you. Understand?" Waste of my breath. It's like when you try to get a pit bull off your face. You hit, punch, and elbow them, just making them angrier.

The thing about OC is that I don't want to be considered an OC person. Nothing is appealing to me about these people whatsoever. Even if I lived in San Diego, it would be more relaxed than living "behind the Orange Curtain." Why does everyone have to be so pretentious? They even have a reality tv show called *The Real Housewives of Orange County*. I wondered what the fake ones would be like. Lord knows they wouldn't have to change the cast. I have never watched the show, but I looked them up out of curiosity because I mentioned them in this book. Here's what I found. None of them are what I would define as particularly gorgeous. They were probably smart or funny or something. They all went to the same plastic surgeon, or the plastic surgeons went to the same school. One of the housewives left the show; she realized it was tough out there and returned. I could have asked Cher about it but decided against it. After all, China did own Hollywood. After returning to the show, she showed off her abs so everyone knew age had not been her foe. It was impressive that each of the ladies was involved in business dealings. Still most had wealthy husbands who could back them in business. The publishers wrote of their net worth. Since they didn't have an exact number for a couple divorcing (no surprise there), that couple was selling their home for $975,000, which decided it. According to the publishers, their net worth was $1,000,000. Ingenious!

I am a housewife in Orange County, and here is the last place I want to be. I am bicoastal, and we are genuinely different people cut from a different cloth. When people say we are all the same, scream "bullshit" as I do. It's not true. We say it like it is, and we stand in our truth. At least my friends and I do. If you don't want to know the truth, please don't ask us. We will tell you most delicately and lovingly. But it will be honest to gawd truth. Now let's get back to the phonies.

I have never seen the show. But if it is like what I know to be accurate, there is a lot of backbiting, who's sleeping with whose husband, who is sticking the knife to whom, and who can keep up with the Joneses. If those are your aspirations, then this is the show for you! Winner, winner, winner! My gay friend, Matt, even told me to buy this shampoo and conditioner. "The 'Real Housewives of Orange County' use it. It 'smellzzz delisshhezz.'" You know what, I bought it because he swore it was the best he had ever used. I bought it, not because these pretentious phonies bought it. I must say, however, he was right. I'll let you in on another little secret. I don't even have to work! It's true! I don't have to work! Especially being an underpaid sweeper. But how would I ever get the comedic entertainment value to write this book?

When I authored this book, In-N-Out Burger paid $50 for an interview and $18 an hour to work. The country is in desperate need for workers. Unemployment is making it too easy for workers to stay home. It's the Bernie Sanders way of life in Vermont. The checks are more than they take home in regular wages. But there is one thing we sweepers shared, and that was loyalty. We stayed loyal at $14 an hour, with a final increase of $15 an hour. The sky is the limit.

As you can tell, I'm not your average OC housewife, and I do not wear yoga pants. My husband is from Palos Verdes. I dress for work as if I were in a fashion show. I am completely and utterly couture, and my nickname is Fashionista. By the way, on the third day of the job, I got rid of the vest. I never wore that felonious vest again. When asked about it, I said it was lost, and they'd give me another. Something has got to be better than believing I'm a felonious super sweeper. Just two years before this, I was in corporate America. I have my BA in business administration. I had a house on the water, a jaguar, and a condo in Florida, and I gave it all up to marry the man of my dreams, put up with Newsome, and become a super sweeper! I need to get off the subject because I'm beginning to feel fecking ill.

I turn to my right and see a boy planting his meatballs in the garden. No, it wasn't a doo-doo, boy. But it just as well could have been. His name will forever be known as "Meatball Man." I sing to him with a chorus sound of "Macho Man" until he pleads for me to stop. And do you know what happens next? He begged for me to sing it to him once I did stop. Oy vey, how do parents do this thing called parenting? As you might have noticed, I'm not a parent. Nor have I ever wanted to be until I married my husband. I have had too much fun in my life. I've done everything I've dreamed of doing, which didn't include having children. You might have even wondered why I want to be an early childhood education teacher. Because I love children. I love to play with children. I love the wonderment in their eyes when they "get it" through a fictional story or a building block. When they'd come up to me and give me a hug, it was the highlight of my day just because they felt a closeness. They can see it in my eyes and read my heart that I care for them. And that's what kept me coming back. And let's not forget the fodder.

Thursdays were always hell for the supervisors. And we weren't sure why, but it wasn't good. The children were just spinning, rocking, and rolling, almost uncontrollably. We blamed it on being a day away from the weekend. Hell, there had to be something else to it. Bingo, as I looked at their breakfast. Holy crap! Sugarcoated waffles. They had so much sugar coating that they would send them on a methamphetamine trip for at least an hour or two. I'm speaking about hitting each other, throwing food, not sitting in their assigned seats, taking their masks off, and screaming in each other's faces. It was any supervisor's nightmare, apart from the privileged peers at the neighboring campus. They have never faced a day like this, nor will they ever have to.

It takes a village to raise a child.
—African Proverb

I decided to take it upon myself to go into human resources and tell David what was happening. David was a bit of a nervous type. He searched for paper and what I now refer to as the invisible ink pen. He wrote down my observation and seemed very interested in my hypothesis. I was very pleased with myself as I turned and walked away. This was what they needed to hear, feedback from the student supervisors. Besides, aren't I the smartest of the smartest supervisors? Dot is intelligent too, but she has Jesus giving her the answers daily; she has an advantage. That makes her disqualified; she doesn't need to think of her own volition.

This reminds me, I have a friend called Laura. I call her Laura because that's her name. She is my spiritual guru. We pray together and work spiritually together. If I'm upset or feel like I'm going to lose it, I go to Laura. Laura, to me, is my rock. She is my human-soul sister. And what's creepy is that Laura knows when I'm trying to skirt an issue or omit something I should be telling her. An omission is the same thing as a lie, she told me. I have a "belly barometer" that I can't live comfortably with when I lie. It's like drinking poison for me. I must get it out and tell the truth. Laura sees through that immediately. I believe we can have soulmates as females, just as we have them as males. God sends many messengers. When he can't speak to us, he sends people who can. Prayer is talking to God; meditation is listening. Laura and I meditate together, and sometimes, the answers come when I'm open to it. Not in my time but in God's time. So I give him five minutes.

This should undoubtedly land me that promotion. David would certainly see to it. I tell Laura. Laura looked at me and didn't say a word, and I honestly hated that because I already knew what she was thinking. She's handing me a bat, metaphorically speaking, so I can use it on my ego. What, what? I asked her. She said nothing. C'mon, tell me!

"Penny, you are forcing your will once again. If you are supposed to have a teaching job, you will have it. You can stamp your feet if you are not supposed to have one. Believe that if there is a different path for you, whatever that may be, it will be the best for you and for your growth spiritually, mentally, and emotionally. Let it go. It will happen. Whatever is supposed to happen will happen for you, my dear Penny. C'mon, let's pray."

I knew it, I knew it, I knew it. Why does Laura always make sense? What if this teaching is not for me? Maybe that's why the walls kept being thrown up. I know God will throw you a stop sign and another stop sign; if you don't stop, he will throw you a brick wall. "Stop forcing your will, Penny."

The following Thursday, I saw the cuties had been thrown around along with the raisin boxes. Hmmm. It can't be the waffles because I specifically told David…they were staring right up at me, those goddamn sugar waffles. And purple paws already had a few stashed away for the family.

Since the pandemic, the teacher's union had decided they wouldn't work until the coast was clear. This only meant the pandemic was not under control, but what they really meant was that COVID was practically nonexistent.

I don't think COVID-19 could reach Hawaii or the Bahamas, so it was more than safe for the teachers to go there for freedom from COVID because that's where the news correspondents found them.

Orange County and California, overall, were open for business.

Don't get me wrong, my sister works harder than anyone I've met in education. She has her doctorate but prefers the classroom. She also teaches college courses online. I have nothing against teachers taking a well-deserved vacation.

ADVENTURES OF A BOUGIE NEW YORKER

President Barack Obama saw the writing on the wall early on. He knew how much harder this field was going to get. Every teacher was given $5,000 when he signed the No Child Left Behind Act."

While the teachers were on holiday, the student supervisors sat in on the extended learning classes. This I found more up my alley. After all, I am a cum laude graduate, just if you hadn't read that earlier. This was my bag. I adored my students in the classes that I saw on a daily schedule. The first class was second graders, and the second class was fourth graders. The second graders were sometimes a handful, but I liked to hear them read to me, and I also liked reading. The first week of the presidential inauguration, I asked the fourth-grade class if they knew our new president's name. Most knew, but one boy yelled, "I wanted Trump to win." I supposed this is what he heard at home. Naturally, we moved on to the next subject. The boys in this class had a hard time sitting down and reading. If it wasn't the one time they all had to go to the bathroom the same day, it became every day. As soon as I walked into class, I heard, "Can I go to the bathroom? Can I go after Samson? Can I go after Carson? Can I go after Connor?" Finally, I started getting used to this game. I said "no," not until the teacher returned.

I then heard, "Oooooh, that was bad, Carson."

I said, "Connor, what did Carson say?"

"I can't tell you because it was really bad, and I'm not allowed to say it."

"Tell me, Carson, what did you say?"

Connor busted out, "He called you a boomer."

"Now what in the world is that?"

"It's just a bad word."

"Connor, what does it mean?"

"It means you're an old lady like a grandma."

"Connor, I didn't say that," said Carson.

"Yes, you did!"

"Look, the teacher is back. See you guys tomorrow," I said. It didn't bother me much because what grandmother looked like me? It's laughable.

The next day, same class, again, Connor started the same call of the wild. "Can I go to the bathroom?" This went on three times a day just in that one class. Then it was "Can I take a buddy?" The assistant teacher told me that Connor was not allowed to have a buddy because he was caught playing in the bushes. Hmmm, good to know.

Once again, "Ms. Penny, can I go to the bathroom?"

"Connor, you need to see a medical doctor. But go ahead."

The following day, Connor came to class and asked to go to the bathroom before sitting down. I said, "Connor, you need to see a medical doctor."

He said, "I told my mother you said that."

Oh boy, here it comes, my first penalty. Dammit, dammit, dammit.

"Oh, okay. What did your mom say?"

"She wanted to know what you looked like and if you had blond hair. And, and, if you were really a teacher."

"Oh, but I am a teacher."

"Well, that's what she wanted to know."

Shite, shite, shite, shite. How dare he blow up my spot. Spoiled brat. What if I were really concerned that he had a urinary tract infection? She should be thanking me instead of playing Columbo. What will she come to the class with a trench coat and ole Doc Robert in tow? Where's my gawd damn thank you!

Connor O'Leary was my favorite student, unbeknownst to him. He was the class clown, and boy, was he funny. Not only did he make the class laugh, but he also made me laugh. I had to hide my laughter because it was hard to keep him in his seat and stop him from talking, even if it were to himself. The choices were either you read, or you were on your computer. Period. At twenty after 2:00 p.m., you could then start drawing on what you read. Yeah, right. That never worked. It was always the "Can I go to the crapper?" or "Connor, please get back to your seat and sit it, else ole Doc Robert has a nice comfy chair in his office just waiting for you. Connor, stop talking. Connor, read to yourself, Connor, Connor, ad infinitum."

Carson spoke up. He said, "Ms. Penny, some girl spit in Connor's face today at recess when we played soccer."

"Connor, is that true?"

"Yes."

"Why did that girl spit on you?"

"Because, well, I was winning, and she didn't like it, so she spit on me."

"Did you tell anybody?"

"No."

"Do you know who she is?"

"No."

"Will you be able to point her out to me tomorrow at recess?"

"Yes, I think so."

"Okay, then tomorrow it is."

While I might have forgotten, *(That should have been caught).*

Carson hadn't. Carson and Danny came running over to me and said they found the girl who spat on Connor. I threw down my broom (not really, but it adds drama) and followed the boys to where the girl was standing. I blew my whistle, pointed to her, and told her to come over to me, curling my pointer finger. Then I asked the boys to get Connor. Connor came and seemed very bashful. This gal must have been a grade above him. She sure looked like she was. I asked her name and if she spat on this boy. And guess what she said? Her name was Donna, and "no," she did not spit on Connor. No surprise there. Connor didn't look up but dug a hole with the top of his sneaker in the dirt.

I said, "You know what? I think you did, so come with me."

Carson and Danny followed us joyfully to watch someone being sent to the principal's office or, in their mind, burned at the stake. But I had to send them back to the playground. I put Donna in a chair outside the assistant principal's office, which always seemed like a dead man walking to the students and letting Assistant Principal Deanna manage her first. I knocked on Deanna's door and peeked my head in. She had the same girl she had every other day, the cutie thrower and the same gal who liked to throw others' lunches in the trash, so that's no big deal. But I will tell you this, she is sharper than a tool. She knows what she's doing when she does it but will look you squarely in the eye and tell you, "No, I didn't do it."

Deanna stepped out and told her privately about the incident, (which should be taken very seriously due to COVID-19), and let her know where Donna was sitting. She asked where Connor was and said she would oversee it from here.

It wasn't but two weeks later, we were down to one person on the field to watch over the children at recess. It was not unusual that there were two grades on the field or playground at any given time. Funnel has been absent a lot lately. I don't think she made it through a week without missing a day that month. This put a lot of pressure on all of us. I don't think she knew any better or didn't care. Either way, it's terrible to be that shorthanded. After all, we kept being told they were filling more positions, but who wanted the job at the rate they were paying? Inflation was rearing its ugly head only to worsen in time.

Plus, you haven't read who else shared the grounds with us. I was going to surprise you, but here it comes, the YMCA! All true. Someone from the YMCA got even mouthier than he already was and was sentenced to another school. As an afterthought, even the YMCA makes more money than us, and they don't have to sweep. We borrow their people sometimes to help but, truthfully, they don't help. They stand around and pretend they're busy. Have you ever met people like that? They can act busy doing nothing, but it looks like they know what they're doing.

All the personnel at the schools carried radios. It was necessary, and it was surreal. I was picking up carrots off the floor and heard, "Nurse, please come to the field with a wheelchair." Lo and behold, Connor was getting wheeled back to the nurse's office with a piece of his scalp left on the soccer net. You'd think some white person performed an atrocity and scalped that damn kid, for feck's sake. I mean, there was an inch of meat hanging on the bar of that net. Connor was the bravest kid I've seen in that school. I yelled to him, "Connor, it's going to be okay, buddy!" (Yeah, sure, if you mean looking like the Native American Indian character in *One Flew over the Cuckoo's Nest*.) He looked at me and waved as the blood streamed down his face. Many of his friends were crying as if it was happening to them. I consoled them and assured them he would get a few stitches and everything would be okay. At least, I hoped so. Who knew if that was his frontal lobe on the bar?

I heard over the loudspeaker, "Pablo, can you get the net out of there and clean it up?"

The girls and I looked at each other, and each of us thought at the same time, now that sounds very suspicious.

The weekend passed, and Connor was back at school the following Monday. His mom wasn't too interested in me any longer. Her loss because I'm a lot of fun once you get to know me.

Getting back to the radios. We were getting things back to their "norm" before the pandemic. It was time for the balls to come out. Basketballs, kickballs, and volleyballs. After recess, the balls were placed in a bin, dumped on the ground, and sprayed with the almighty viricide. This was another task for the super sweepers. Since we weren't given instructions on cleaning the balls, I questioned Deanna over the radio, "Deanna, how are we supposed to scrub the balls?" (*Crickets.*)

We had this groovy janitor, Pablo. He was so cool and could outdance Michael Jackson any day of the week. I mean, if Michael were alive. He is not an eyesore either; I saw the ladies giggle like high school girls, making it even more pleasant to have him around. I swear it. "He got the moves." But don't take advantage of him because he won't tolerate it. I never had a problem with Pablo. I have seen people who have, and they were never impolite to him again. He was nobody's fool. One day, the super sweepers were all sitting around on break. We heard a teacher, Whatsherbucket, radio to Pablo that there is a cockroach in the classroom and asked if he could come to get it. Pablo retorted that he was too busy right now. One of the students clogged the bowls with toilet paper, and Pablo was called. Afterward, Pablo locked the bathroom door, and Funnel radioed him to tell him Red was locked in the bathroom and could not get out. Pablo asked if Funnel was sure he was in the bathroom. Funnel was not specific. Pablo said she'd better be sure before he made a trip back there. I saw ole Doc Robert coming, running, around the corner with his key. Red was not in there, by the way.

Another morning, I heard a radio go off, and Whatsherbucket got on and said, "A student just threw his laptop across the room," and we have exited the classroom. I wondered if he was aiming it at her. Sheez, so formal.

Next, I heard Doc Robert over the speaker, saying, "C'mon, Jason, will you get out of my bushes." He may have gotten out because I don't think he would have slept there.

On Monday, I saw a crowd of students and teachers looking up over the lunch area onto the roof. I wondered what was going on. There I saw Pablo carefully scaling the top of the school's roof. I yelled, "Pablo, it is not worth it."

"Nothing is if you have children!"

Before I could convince him of anything else, a ball came rolling down the roof then another and another. I abruptly turned around, walked so fast into the staff bathroom, and waited in the stall until I could catch my breath. I kept taking deep breaths, telling myself to play like it was a joke. It was a joke, Penny. Think about it. It's funny. Like he's going to take his life 18 feet from the ground. Stop being so hard on yourself. It's funny. Now get out of here and hold your head up high. Start sweeping.

Not long after that, I saw Pablo, started laughing uncomfortably, and said, "Hey, now they got you on the roof rescuing balls."

"Yeah," he said. "And I'm never doing it again."

The school hired another super sweeper, Sassy. Her post is on the hot concrete watching the children play. Keep an eye out. It was days before I saw what Sassy looked like. I swear on everything I own (and that's a lot) that she wore Hannibal Lecter's mask in *Silence of the Lambs*. It was so unbecoming. Man, can it get hot out there? I am not one to sit out in the sun. I would simply have to refuse. The sun is not suitable for me, and I feel like I will pass out, which will not do in my expensive clothes. And this job is not buying them, trust me when I tell you. Back to Sassy.

Sassy had a daughter who misbehaved. She thought it best to work at the school to keep her in check. I supposed she couldn't afford for a child psychologist to know that it's obvious it's because of you, Sassy, that the child screwed up in the first place. That's where I would start. Doesn't that sound like a good place, Sassy? Or you're just a Joan Crawford type and get paid to ensure your wayward child keeps her mouth shut. You did tell me when she saw you, she cried. Put me in front of a judge. I would say the very same thing to them. In fact, all the supervisors have or had children at the school. It makes sense. In Sassy's first week, she's caught handing out jawbreakers to the kids. Doc Robert walked around, asking who was giving the kids jawbreakers. I just figured her husband was an oral surgeon, which was a perfect way to get good business. Wise woman, resolute wife/child abuser.

Sometimes, at odd hours at night, we would get some undecipherable texts from Funnel. One time, she read an article about a man killed fighting off some guy trying to kidnap or do something heinous to his girlfriend. She wanted us to donate to a man we had never met or even had the whole story about. It was a news clip that was shown on a local news channel. Funnel wrote that she would drive to LA herself and donate to his family. I don't know how she would get the address, but she also wanted to throw a tennis tournament to benefit the family. Now Funnel had just had a knee operation three months prior, which made her unable to do many things the super sweepers had to do, like moving a muscle. I wondered if the tournament benefit was for us to do. None of which I was remotely interested in. I asked her to just put together a GoFundMe page. I never heard another word about it.

Another time we got an indecipherable text. This time I wrote back. Excuse me? She had fallen ill and had been hospitalized for pneumonia. She was just trying to get her memory back. And to beware that we might see postings in her area that she has gone missing. Did she post postings of herself lost? Did she put herself on the milk cartons? I'll never know. Here's what I imagined, "I'm lost. Here's a picture of me. If you see me, call me on my number 867-5309. I don't know my name or where I live. But thanks for calling." I haven't heard from her in a while, so I think she found herself. Maybe she saw a poster and called the number. The person on the other end told her where to go.

There are just so many things.

Get this, seven student supervisor spots are carved out for us in the parking lot. It's kept hush-hush until Cher and Paula get to know you well enough to let you on the "know". Dot found out after a month of leaving her brand-new Mercedes on the busy road and walking to the school. She made it a point to tell me, and she sure did. That makes four of us because Funnel wasn't quick to offer the information. I was busting a hump for a while, leaving my new car on the busy road. I even asked the nervous HR man, David, if there were any spots to park my car, and he told me there weren't any left.

"None left? David, why in your world does seven minus five equal zero?"

"Because my calculation is seven minus five equals two. Maybe that's why I didn't get a raise."

David hadn't figured it out. Now I get it. It's not his fault at all. I just needed him to figure it out. I decided to leave notes, "Thanks for visiting our school. Now this is someone's parking spot. Please don't park here again." I paraphrased. These snotty bastids continued to do it. I didn't care any longer. I just parked wherever I wanted to, just like "them." After all, I probably had one of the nicest cars there. Finally, the assistant principal, Deanna, sided with us and sent an announcement to our friendly neighbors who had been parking in our spots; they stopped for a while. Perverting the justice course began again, so we placed cones in our spots. These bastids moved our cones to park their cars. Now there was no other recourse but to sit and wait. We all took our posts.

"Aha, just as we suspected!"

"Well, we are all the same."

"To hell we are. You make more money. And we sweep!"

"Touché."

It did not happen again. We had to get tough.

I decided I would need to push myself to a more challenging position. It just wasn't happening quite as quickly as I had imagined. I made an appointment to see the human resources manager/office manager. I brought my transcript (innovative thinking) and handed it to David. David perused the script, said a few nice things, and handed it back. I pushed it slowly across the desk back toward him while locking my gaze on him. That sarcastic smile crept across his face. He told me he was late for a meeting with Dr. Robert; he congratulated me on a well-done job. He stood up to indicate the meeting was over while handing me my transcript. It takes me a lot to feel anger, but isn't that always the first emotion?

What! You are supposed to keep this in your filing cabinet. Or hand this to your manager next door. What's wrong with you, people? Don't you see a prize winner when they walk through the door? That's it. I'm boycotting sweeping for the day. And to tell you the truth, it was never on the job description, to begin with. Brooms were just left as a subtle hint. We took it, and sixty percent of our job became sweeping from day one. Yes, I could have stood there like a prima donna and let the other girls sweep and never picked up the broom and just observed like I was told to do. But how is that being a team player?

Yes, I'm better than everyone on my team, but do I have to flaunt it? If Jesus can clean feet, I can pick up a broom. I consider it a lesson in humility. You can see Dot is working on me. Dot doesn't need to work, either. I think her absolute dream is to build a church. I'm pretty sure she's drawn the blueprints. I don't ask too many questions as she thinks I'm poking fun at this stage. I've pushed it that far.

Look, I must laugh. Even if it's at another's expense, so be it. Gawd, why do people have to be so sensitive? Hell, I was called a boomer! I'm not going to keep bingo, Alzheimer's, or the fact that when you dust, be careful because it may be me, out of my conversations. I have been known to say, "Focus on your fabulousness, not on your flaws." My sense of humor makes me fabulous, darling. It is far from a deficiency. Soon you will realize that Dot, like all the others!

The teacher's union agreed that the teachers were coming back to the classrooms. The pandemic had run its course. This ruins everything. These teachers were not OC. Nope, no way. Most of them were out of shape. The airlines were trying to recoup what finances they lost with the pandemic. They decided to charge obese/overweight tomayto/tomahto person(s) more money to fly. I imagined how it went: "Hey, you, next in line, pick up your bag and get over here and stand on this meat scale. Er, yup, just what I was thinking. Wait over here. Sally, bring that register over here now. We gotta tally this one up. I think this one's gonna need a row."

That was my new game. To count the people who would give the money back to the airlines. Genius David will be gifting his bonus to the airline fund. Good business. It will save me money in the long run. Newsome is taxing us up the ying-yang.

Hopefully, there'll be enough people to push the eject button on him soon. I know they have my signature.

There was but one teacher that wasn't back…yet. This teacher was at the Capitol on the day of the alleged "insurrection." Dare I say it? People saw his grill on the television, so his presence was not welcome until he was cleared of any wrongdoing. I was asked to supervise his accelerated classroom occasionally, and these kids were way out of my league. I mean uncontrollable. They performed cartwheels, threw popcorn, played on their devices, laughed, and carried on when I first walked in. I couldn't get over it. How long has this been going on? And to add insult to injury, I had these same kids, but even more of them, if you can imagine, in another class. I couldn't find a practical way to find some control over them. Nobody could. It was a mutiny on the bounty. I heard later that they liked their teacher, which was their way of acting out.

I would write these kids up with pink slips for the teachers, and they would just thank me. I let these kids out ten minutes early for recess because of the games that went on, the basketball, fake news, and whatever they found on their computers; I just couldn't keep track. While one distracted me, someone else was up to some other shenanigans. They made "Welcome back, Kotter" look like prep school kids. There were times that Deanna used to come into the class to speak softly and slowly enough for me to try to keep my eyes open. This was her way of trying to calm them down. It worked until she left. And then the action started again. This is what Dr. John Robert meant by "entitled brats." I saw it with my very own eyes.

Whenever there was a problem with students in the field or lunchroom, the super sweepers came to me. They knew that I was tough on them and had every right to be. They were sneaky. I wrote them up every chance I got. I split them up at tables. I made them sit out for a short time during recess because somebody had to do it. They tried to make our lives miserable at times, and I wouldn't have it. I'm speaking about the fourth and fifth graders mainly. Again, they would purposely dump their trays of food on the floor right before lunch was over, but eight out of ten times, I would catch them because I would not stop until I did. Then I would pull them off the field and make them sweep it up. It was "never" theirs naturally, but they were more than willing to sweep up whomever it was.

The following day, I would see who was at that table. I would take another perpetrator and sit them at a different table, teaching them loyalty to a friend. They understood never to allow a friend to take the rap. I was not well-liked, and I didn't care. These kids were not going to give me more sweeping that I wasn't supposed to be doing in the first place. It was eighty degrees, and the water fountain wasn't working again.

The other sweepers were starting to catch on. Nice did not make your job easier; discipline did. Pablo loved what we had been doing because the floors were clean at the end of our shift, and the tables were cleared off. We began dismissing the students, but not until we made sure their table was clear and the floor was clean underneath their table. Some gawd damn students would take the back route just to leave their mess, but come hell or high water, I'd find the rat fink from the group who loved to tattle. I learned that children loved to squeal. They lived for it. They will inform you right before the perpetrator, who could be their best buddy, which I found amusing. They could be standing so close to one another that they would be touching arms, and sum bitch, their finger would point right at them just to say who did it. Then they'd run off together and play on the field.

That reminds me of my close friend Mary. Mary used to say, "A real friend doesn't come to the pokey to bail you out. A real friend is sitting right next to you in handcuffs." I liked that analogy.

One time, Pablo came back to the lunch tables while we were getting ready to go, and he was screaming. I've never heard him this angry before. Some smart alecks had left a mess of utter shit piled high from the table to the awning ceiling. Now I asked if they weren't not picking it up, who was? Nonconforming bastids. Pablo radioed Doc Robert, and ole Doc Robert called the kids back to clean it up. He pulled Pablo aside and said he couldn't let the kids get to him. Yeah, right. These disrespectful sum bitches take it with a grain of salt. Sounds like a plan. And the mothers, oh the OC mothers, will call Dr. John Robert and Deanna if their child gets a pink slip for playing invisible basketball in class. It's the non-teacher-teacher's fault, and we're brave enough to be there! As I suspected, there was a handwritten note on my radio charger: "Penny, can I talk to you before you leave?"

Here we go. *Knock, knock, knock.*

"Come in. Oh, hi, Penny. Please have a seat," said our human resources director, David. "I had a conversation today with a highly upset mother, and I wondered if you knew anything about it."

Oh, here we go, I thought.

"Did you tell Hayden that she was the worst student in the class?"

I smirked and said, "Yes, David, I did."

"Can you tell me why you would say such a thing?"

"Well, as you probably know already, I have a keen sense for teaching, and when a child, or ahem, privileged child, cannot sit in her seat, won't listen, and tells me "no", I do have a problem with that. The other students are thoughtful, hand in their work at the end of the class, and follow drawing instructions. They are excellent students. When Hayden hands in a picture and calls it, "Teacher" and it looks like an apple left out in the sun. I did think the "worst student" in the class was an ideally perfect name. She deserves to wear the worst student pin."

"Just a word to the wise, Ms. Penny, Orange County parents will not tolerate that behavior."

"Excuse me, Mr. David, it is not my behavior we should be looking at. Good night, Mr. David."

It was a crisp March morning, and I watched the children play on the basketball courts. This was my first stint of the day. I spotted Connor wearing a deep green sweater with olive pants. I could never miss Connor because of his flaming red hair.

As usual, he was roughhousing with the other boys. I remembered walking over to the other supervisors, and out of the corner of my eye, I saw a van with those creepy black-tinted windows surrounding it. I hate those trucks and vans, and they are all over as of late. I will not park or walk next to one. If "defunding the police" wasn't the "in" thing today, I would get signatures for the police officers to stop every one of the vans, trucks, and cars in which the owners disguise themselves. It is weird, and at the same time, it is meant to intimidate. It used to be against the law, but there aren't many law enforcement peace officers around to uphold it. It makes my blood boil.

The van left the grounds the same way a food truck or repair truck would come or go. I thought it odd that nobody really paid attention to it. I hear all those amber alerts on my phone a lot of the time. I admit I am paranoid. But once the amber alert goes off on your phone and you see the helicopters, you will never forget the prayers you hear yourself saying aloud.

The kidnapping for sex trafficking with the border of Mexico being so close needs to be taken seriously. The border is something to fear when women and children come in to play. I often wondered how mothers could let their children play outside unattended for hours, never checking on them, assuming everything was right with the world. And I love how smug people get when they smile and say, "Oh, I don't watch the news. It's too depressing." I know you don't. You're a dumb arse because if you did, you wouldn't let your blond hair, blue-eyed girls run around this complex daily while you're at work, and they have no supervision.

"Oh, what's that, Jen?" She's crying to my husband. "You can't find Sara, and you just know something terrible has happened? Well, Jaysus, Mary, and Joseph, Jen, what would make you think that?"

My dear husband said to Jen, "Okay, you go this way. I'll go that way." After five minutes, they both met back, and Jen was shaking Sara, crying, her voice cracking, saying, "Do you know what could have happened?"

"No, Jen, I think you have that backward. Do you know what could have happened? Perhaps somebody could have needed an organ that day. Or even stranger, adrenochrome, a drug created by the adrenaline of frightened children, used by a satanic child trafficking ring who wanted the blood to keep their youth. Child pornography is always a seller for those pedophiles that live in your neighborhood. We all remember hearing about Jeffrey Epstein and his companion Ghislaine Maxwell which was shocking. The well-to-do Manhattanites. Feel free to look them up. It is appalling and disgraceful."

Well, hallelujah! We have opened borders with over six million immigrants and counting that have crossed. Less police, more criminals, less detection, more murderers, rapists, child molesters, higher taxes, high gasoline prices, higher heating and electric bills, food bills, and more variant viruses and fentanyl deaths.

Yet we are mandated to get COVID shots and wear masks, but many are still getting COVID. We are finished with our fifth booster. Don't ask me. Seems everyone is held harmless. Pharmaceutical companies are rich, China is richer, and Fauci has retired. At the same time, the immigrants just walk in, spreading their diseases. Thank you, Mr. President. Are we now living in the Build Back Better era? I sure didn't think anything was goddamn broken! Until now. We will be "Venezuela" in no time. And the shite is getting worse. Food is becoming scarce on the shelves. We are now declaring war on Russia while handing over $45 billion to Ukraine. This is just the beginning. I remember hearing stories about how my great-grandmother washed her aluminum foil, saved her bacon grease, and reused her teabags during the Great Depression. I hope I'm not waiting to find out.

When recess is over, the children all line up on their colored dots for their teachers to pick them up to bring them to their classrooms. This is when we, super-duper sweepers, take our break. I felt something bothering me in the pit of my stomach. But I wasn't going to embarrass myself as I did when I told Pablo not to throw himself off the flipping roof 18 feet down. Not going through that again. Forget it.

Connor, Come Back

"I don't see Connor. Where's Connor? For feck's sake, where is Connor? Dot, Paula, Sassy, Cher, Paula, somebody, have you seen Connor?"

"I just saw him a few minutes ago."

"How long ago?"

"Well, when he was playing with those boys," said Sassy.

"Dot, Cher! Have you seen Connor?"

"No," they said in unison. "Not in a while."

"Please help. Connor was here, and there was a van, and now he's not. Check the bathrooms, but don't say anything until we are sure. Please, now! In the meantime, I will walk past Ms. Deirdre's class to see if he's in his seat."

I ran down aisles of classrooms as fast as I could to get to Ms. Deirdre's. I investigated through the window and caught students' eyes looking at me. Shoot. Didn't want to draw attention. But there I saw it, an empty seat with Connor's book bag next to his chair. I just wanted to cry. Please, God, no, no.

"Cher, Sassy, Paula, anyone, did you find him?"

"No. Should we alert Dr. Robert? Did anyone check the nurse's office?"

"Let me do it," said Dot. "In the meantime, I'll go check the theater and library. The rest of you search the parking lot, YMCA, and our neighbors. We are losing time."

We all met back at the tables in three minutes. That's all we have. Three minutes. They could be in Oceanside by now.

We all came back, wiping our eyes. It's time. In a single file, we moved like a dead man walking to his final demise. His door was shut. I knocked on it and opened it. Deanna was in there as well as David. Perfect. Doc Robert gave me the one-minute sign, and I shook my head no. Now finger pointed down. He looked at me with bugged eyes and waved us to come in. I started, "Dr. Robert, is there any reason we should suspect Connor O'Leary's whereabouts aren't known? Ms. Penny, can you please explain?"

"Dr. Robert, I was watching Connor this morning at recess. I saw a black van drive away from the corner of my eye. When the children lined up for class, I noticed that Connor wasn't in line. I searched for him in the bathrooms, Ms. Deirdre's classroom, the—"

"Ms. Penny, do you mean to tell me you waited until now to tell me that you cannot find Connor? David, get on the radio and order a lockdown!"

"Well, uh, yes, sir. I wanted to make sure that—"

"David, get 911 on the phone and tell them we may have a missing person[s] at Newport District School. Please send the peace officers right away. George and Penny, would you say this would be out of character for Connor to disappear like this?"

"For as long as I have been Connor's XL teacher, Connor likes his classmates and school. There is no reason to believe Connor would not attend class. I'm afraid this is not the norm. When I noticed his book bag, I knew something was wrong."

"George, please radio Ms. Deirdre and meet with me in my office. Have her assistant take over her class. Thank you. Penny, can you tell me more about the van."

"It was a black van, like a delivery van. It had black-tinted windows, which you could not see through. And a paper license plate."

"Did you get all that?"

"My name is Dr. John Robert, and I am the principal at Newport Elementary School. Not for long, I am thinking. You are inundated with video equipment all over your office. You are a phony. What will the parents say when they speak with WYXN Broadcast Station for Orange County? You will have to move Doc Robert out of state and, by god, change that horrible first-last name, for god's sake. And grab a broom on the way out. You may need a fresh start."

The school was winding down for summer vacation. There were whispers all around the office.

I tried my hardest to listen in, but it was too muffled even for my impeccable hearing. Connor was not back. The desk in Ms. Deirdre's office was moved so the students could take their minds off Connor's absence for a while. That was all that was said, mums the word. I fell deeper and deeper into depression as I realized how much I adored this boy and how the world had failed me. How people have forgotten me and now, the entire country. It came to the point that I was either living for my life or for my death. I was spiraling down, and my husband was worried. I knew I needed help.

That's when I met Dr. Corona (not even kidding). He asked me why I was here, and I couldn't get a word out because I cried and cried that I missed life. I forgot life the way it was. Watching children riding their bikes, children playing outdoors, swinging on swings, knocking on my door for Halloween treats, and now it was all bitter memories. I saw masks hiding everyone's identity, personalities, and souls. I reckon if you had a good soul, you could see it in one's eyes. That was few and far between. The world had gone mad. Lockdowns and shut-ins were the new norms. Death and destruction had taken over. Australia told their citizens not to even talk to their neighbors. They were so controlled by this coronavirus. The CDC (Crazy Dumbass Cornballs) had a new plan every month, and yet none of it was working. People were dying, especially the seniors. I told Dr. Corona about Connor. And that is when I lost it. Dr. Corona was speechless. The man had a heart. I knew he knew what I was talking about. I also knew he must have been sick of all the wisecracks over his name. Everyone is a comedian.

He gave me a few prescriptions and told me to call him in a few days, that it would take a week to feel that something was working to make me feel "better." He was right. I realized then that you could mask the sadness but simply can't make it disappear.

Reflection

"Joe Biden has allowed migrants from 181 countries to enter our country, some of which have opened their prisons and have dumped their most heinous criminals onto the USA. Different cartels and MS-13 gang members have somehow gotten through. Cartels are running their drugs from the southern border now, which is 933 miles long. It stretches from the Pacific Ocean to the tip of Texas. There is no stopping the amount of fentanyl and opioids on the streets, which, disturbingly, has murdered over 106,000 people in the US alone in 2023. China is supplying the precursor of ingredients to Mexico. Unless something is done, we will be a province of China. It seems to be that their own countries don't want them in their prisons, so they opened their prisons, and now they are coming into our country. They have crossed our border. Child sex trafficking and child pornography are at an all-time high, and it's right here in a few towns over in Anaheim. Less the border is two hours away. Dr. Robert, there is pervasive evilness in this world, and it's right on our goddamn doorstep." These immigrants owe their coyotes for bringing them to the border. The coyotes work for the cartels. Now the immigrants are in indentured servitude. Everyone must be paid, whether through sex trafficking, organ harvesting, human trafficking, or drug trafficking. All are very lucrative businesses. The cartels have become diversified. They no longer rely only on drugs for their revenue stream. "We are not in Kansas anymore."

There was a time when I lived on the east coast that I decided to pick up a hobby. I was sad; I was searching for meaning in my life. I needed to keep myself occupied. I wanted to awaken my spiritual self. I began learning about angels, meditation, and energy-cleansing work. It was 1996, and I would continue this work through 2001. It was neat, and I discovered more truths about the universe, its energies, and myself.

There were steps involved, as in anything learned. I read plenty of books and listened to tapes on meditation, angels, spiritual guides, and energy centers. I read books by Deepak Chopra, Marianne Williamson, Doreen Virtue, Wayne Dyer, Dalai Lama, James Vaan Prague, and Mother Teresa, just to name a few. I was on a search for knowledge and truth. I decided then to teach myself to read tarot cards. I read for my friends and my family. I also cleansed my home and opened my energy chakras through meditation. I found that everyone has a sixth sense. Whether or not they work on it is another thing. It could be that one time that something tells you to slam on the brakes when you just didn't know why, but you were so relieved you did. Or you saw a relative that transitioned many years before. Something will happen in your life that will make you believe we are humans having a spiritual experience. But if you're not ready for it, don't ask for it. We often want to see the future; most of the time, the reality is that we don't.

So why are people so excited to go to a tarot reader or psychic? I would think it's only four concrete reasons: (1) to find out if a past lover will return, (2) if one was going to come into money, (3) if one was going to recover from a severe illness, and (4) if a deceased family member was okay. Now imagine if you were a so-called psychic. This stuff is easy breezy. You can guess right away why that man or woman is coming in just by reading the expression on their face. Guessing their age, their energy, and their stance are many dead giveaways. But you give them three questions and start pulling those cards. I venture to think there is a lot of deception in this field. However, and this is very important to understand, many psychics have paranormal and metaphysical psychic abilities. I would advise against ever using a psychic via telephone, it just doesn't work, and you are being taken for the ride of your life.

It was fun for a while to get the answers right. But suddenly, I had dreams about my own life. These dreams were becoming real. They were entering into my reality. Some people think they want to know the future. Be very careful with this; because when you do, it is a spooky experience. It was not bad per se, but it was creepy. I didn't care for it, and thus the end of my stint into the paranormal.

Stefania

However, it did bleed into my neighbor's interest. She has always been a heavy smoker and chain-smoked nearly every time she did the cards. She'd take a puff, shuffle the cards, take a puff, shuffle the cards, etc. However, it became more than an "interest." It became an obsession. To date, she sits in her home, rarely leaving it "puff, puff, shuffle, shuffle" as she lays out her cards. I have not spoken to this person in nine years. She was addicted. She relies solely on what she believes the cards are saying about her life, future actions, and others around her.

Let me back up a bit. When we met, Stefania was beautiful—an American Italian with long shiny, thick brunette hair. She had beautiful big expressive brown eyes, olive skin, an hourglass shape, and clothes right off the rack from Saks—a true Manhattanite. She was a trader at one of the most prestigious global investment banks, and she ranked high on the scales. Every investment bank wanted her, and every man tried to seduce her. Her name is Stefania.

Stefania's family story was almost like a chapter written on genocide. Every member of her immediate family died of cancer except a sister, who remained distant for whatever reason. I now have my suspicions as to why. Maybe she realized that Stefania had gone off the deep end; maybe not.

Stefania and I became fast friends. She came over one night when a bunch of my girlfriends were over having fun reading the cards. Stefania began to tell us how she lived in a building we all knew down the road. She pointed it out and said to us that in the

1990s, it was the "in" building in which to live. However, she continued, she needed to flee that building because an evil male spirit lived and lurked there. She knows this because it visited her almost every day. She spoke of not sleeping in her bedroom because the room would drop down to temperatures in the teens when she did. The man wore a top hat and a cloak, and when he felt like being alone, he would slip under the closet door and stay in there until he was ready to be seen by Stefania again. The description sounded more like Papa Legba, but I said nothing, for who was I to make light of someone's hellacious nightmare? Sometimes, she would come home, and there would be smears of ketchup all over the countertops and shelves. He would dishevel the home in different ways. The chain lock would rattle at night, and something or someone in her head kept telling her to jump off the roof.

From that day forward, she fell from grace. She went from the penthouse views of Manhattan high finance to a chain-smoking, paranoid, delusional, shut-in obsessed with the occult and living in squalor. She adopted movie script stories as part of her personal history. She claimed to have been part of the famous Lufthansa heist depicted in *Goodfellas*. She never got into detail but led me to believe that she was in the actual van, in the crash car, or involved in the entire planning. She continued to behave as if her house and phones were bugged. As if the Feds were going to kick down her door any moment.

Stefania decided to research the building since its reconstruction in the 1990s. She found out it had once been an asylum in the 1950s. This asylum caused many people to jump off the roof and commit suicide. Why? Nobody knows. But what's even odder is that suicides continued even after the rebuild. Even somebody I once knew, who seemed to have their life together, committed the ultimate sacrifice. That somebody swears to have seen him on the boardwalk not too long after his death. A disgruntled soul is an unfulfilled soul.

Stephania's condo 9H earned the moniker 9HELL. It was a condominium that switched hands quite often. After living there for a fleeting time, she broke the lease and bought a house next to mine.

But she told me that soon after she moved in, the man followed her there, and we were not to speak of him inside her house because it would give him strength and power. I was there almost every day and did not see this man, but everyone else she had over said they had seen him for feck's sake.

It was 3:00 a.m. when I got a call from Stefania who was hysterical.

"Penny, Penny, he is here! Please can I come over? I am so scared."

She was crying as I'd never heard before. I hesitated because if I let her in, would she bring that fecking thing with her? Is it going to attach itself to my body and now become one of my pets? This is a serious decision. Do I want that thing living with me? Now I'm in crisis mode. I mean, she did bring this on herself with her uneducated company. "Witches, all of them witches" (*Rosemary's Baby*).

Penny, she was my friend. We must help our friends. I believed in the "no matter what" club. I possessed to have strong faith. Nothing should deter you. Okay, I thought, here goes nothing! Maybe the man would show up with mirrored sunglasses and bust out singing "November Rain." Stefania was being tormented by Slash from Guns and Roses.

Trembling, I opened my door. Stefania stood there without any shadow of a man with a top hat behind her.

"Come in, come in," I told her. I could tell she'd been crying. She told me that the demon gave her sleep paralysis, which meant she lay awake in bed and could not move. All she could do was stare at the ceiling for minutes and hours. I said, "Shhh, let's not talk about it. The more we talk, the more power we give it." I don't know if I was right or wrong, but who needed that thing hanging by my window?

I made a bed for her in my room, but I could not sleep. I stared at her, freaked out, waiting for a shadow with a cloak and top hat.

Fast-forward, Stefania had a very wealthy French boyfriend at this time. The IRS took everything away, the soon-to-be ex-wife took the rest, and he was left penniless. He moved in with Stefania. Two unemployed Americans with a dream now living together. Stefania kept that dream alive through the cards. Every time I visited, she smoked, and I would get this barely audible mantra in my head, "Puff, puff, shuffle, shuffle."

Afterward, she would say, "Do you see it? It's right here, Tomas (toe-MAHS). There are the swords. You're going to get this deal!"

He would look at her with glazed eyes and say, "Yes, Stefania, I see it." What else could he do? He'd be homeless without her. PS. He didn't get the deal.

Things got so bad, according to Stefania, that the goddamn top hat that used to linger at the window, and had become so large that the entire room would go dark.

Stefania would say, "Right, Tomas, didn't it, didn't it?"

Tomas would look at her and say, "Yes, Stefania."

I knew something was wrong with the way he answered her. It was idiotic, catatonic, and robotic. If that happened, there would be a lot of emotion behind that answer. It's asinine.

She also talked in code when on the telephone. And you better know the code names, or you will be completely lost in conversation.

She swore she was bugged, and the FBI listened to her telephone calls. What did I know?

Tomas and Stefania finally got their break. They were leaving for a week to Belgium in the morning. There was some big business deal that was the answer to their prayers. It was all hush-hush, no details. I didn't ask. I decided I was better off.

Two days later, they were back. Hmmm. Something stinks. A week later, I went to visit them. They told me they went to Belgium to meet with some gentleman in their hotel room. The deal is sealed, and this mystery gentleman was to meet them in the morning to sign off on the deal and give them oodles of money, and they would head home. That never happened. The gentleman disappeared. He disappeared! Tomas and Stefania were calling this man off the hook. No answer. They searched high and low. They stayed an extra night for him in case he reappeared. However, to coin a phrase, "it wasn't in the cards." They flew home.

As far as I know, this mystery man has never been seen or heard from again. But his disappearance was not something Stefania could quickly shake. She started obsessively reading the cards. Puff, Puff, Shuffle, Shuffle and sees the man in a cold dark place, a very dark place. She thinks maybe he is the devil or was killed and is buried underground. That's a cold dark place, right?

I don't know how she did it that time, but she met this church-going Catholic girl who was Hispanic; her name was Gabriella. At that time, Stefania's sister had been diagnosed with cancer and didn't have much time to live. Gabriella was at Stefania's house constantly, and they both prayed with rosary beads. The story is about a crucifix flying off the wall and almost hitting Gabriella in the face.

"Correct, Tomas. Didn't that happen?"

"Yes, Stefania."

"It did! It did!" chimed in Gabriella.

Rosemary transitioned soon after that episode, and what I was told by Stefania was that Gabriella called and said, "I'm so happy Rosemary's coming home!"

"Gabriella, Rosemary died."

"Stefania, nooo, I just talked to her. She was watching the Godfather and said she felt great, and the doctors are letting her out tomorrow."

"No, Gabriella, she's dead. She died today. Rosemary is dead! Do you hear me?"

"But it can't be. We just hung up, Stefania. I swear it's true. Call her. Call her now!"

Gabriella and Stefania's friendship didn't last too long. I'm not sure why. I know Stefania called Gabriella at work one day and said, "I know what you're doing, and it had better stop!" I found out that Gabriella was allegedly sacrificing animals across the street from Stefania's house and leaving the animal's remains on her doorstep. Who could blame Stefania for going mad if that were the truth?

Before Stefania's sister Rosemary's diagnosis, we sat in Stefania's living room. Stefania told me after a few glasses of wine that her sweater had gone on fire the night before. Out of nowhere, her sweater just caught fire on her sleeve. "Isn't that right, Rosemary?" Rosemary just turned to her and stared. She didn't say a word. I was impatiently waiting for a response. What seemed like two minutes, possibly only two seconds, but she wouldn't respond. What was going on here? Everything Stefania said, I believed. Why wouldn't I? Why do these imbecilic people just stop and stare like Stefania is crazy? Finally, Rosemary just nodded yes.

Stefania started building a clientele by reading cards. She would take telephone calls from desperate people. Some visited her home and waited outside until she arrived should she be out. These people were not all there psychologically.

They wanted to hear what they wanted to hear, and Stefania would tell them a bit of good news but keep them coming back for more. I remember a woman in the very affluent area on the Northshore of Long Island who swore there was an evil demon in her home. Stefania would have a weekly call to dispel or encourage her feelings. I think it would be the latter since the weekly call was taking place, and the check was always in the mail.

I began to see that Stefania didn't drink every day, but she couldn't stop when she did. Not until she became ossified. Stefania could not control her speech patterns and had become repetitive with her storytelling. I absorbed everything she said, and while most things may have sounded outlandish, who was I to discount or disbelieve what she would say? The problem became that I couldn't ask her a question as a friend without saying, "Let's ask the cards. See what they say." Shuffle, shuffle…

One day, Stefania and I were taking a walk on the boardwalk. Stefania was explaining to me that her family doesn't bleed. What, where, when? In 1986, she was in the hospital with a hammer toe and ready to undergo surgery. She willed the offending toe better, and the doctors and nurses were amazed. I'm not sure how this didn't end up in the medical journals as a case study, but I never asked. Just then, a high-pitched scream came from Stefania.

I said, "OMG, what's going on?"

She said, "Don't worry, it happens sometimes."

"What happens sometimes?"

"A spirit walked through me."

Does that ever happen to you? (*Crickets.*)

It had been a long time since I had seen Stefania; I moved and went on with my life; work, friends, and boyfriends kept me busy. When I finally met up with Stefania about a year later, I remembered being horrified. Stefania looked like a witch, an absolute witch. I kid you not. She had black teeth, long black hair, and pale skin. She had put on weight and was no longer the happy-go-lucky woman I had known and loved. She now had become whatever it was she was after—the witch with the cards.

I began to see that people who don't have these unique gifts and dabble in things they shouldn't don't get wealthy. My thoughts are that they have more bad luck than good and most are suffering from financial insecurity. And physically, they turn into what they set out to portray—a witch. I believe this is called "karmic retribution."

Sassy, Dot, and I made the best of the last couple of weeks. The coach played DJ in Dot's field, and we just danced and sang while I pretended I was riding on my broom. I'm sure the fourth and fifth graders agreed that's where I belonged, as if I gave a crap. They were the spoiled, entitled brats, remember? As soon as I turned my back, they were the ones who dumped their trays on the floor. If I could, I would stick my broom right up their arse.

They called me the fashionista. Of course, I am. It is an obligation to myself and to the entire school because, after all, I am a qualified teacher. I took my accelerated learning class to recess one day, and Dot was doing the same.

She yelled, "Penny, Penny, a boy is climbing over the fence!"

"Oh no, you ain't!" I had the most fabulous long dress on with crocheted orange and brown colors and many dusted sparkles. There was a slip underneath that was more of a nude color. This dress was costly. I took my whistle around my neck and blew as hard as possible, running with my funky long dress toward the scalawag. Neither knew this boy's name, so I called him "Stripes." I called him Stripes because he wore a striped T-shirt. "Stripes, Stripes, get over here!" Now I was damn serious, and I turned around to see Dot laughing so hard that tears were streaming down her face. Then the boy looked down at his clothes and figured out it was him. I tripped and fell into the mud and grass; my dress was nearly over my head. The crochet stretched out, and the slip barely covered my breasts. But was I embarrassed? Hell to the no, why should I be? I just stopped a significant security breach. I felt like a Recon Marine at Gitmo. I had visions of ole Doc Robert pinning a Medal of Valor on my ample chest. And maybe even a Purple Heart.

As I mentioned earlier, they all looked like they chose clothes at the local Salvation Army. I donated there all the time. I keep waiting to see someone wearing a garment I gave away. What a bunch of douzies.

There were two of us who didn't need the yaab mon. That was Dot and me. I decided to go back to school. After all, if you weren't a real union teacher, you would continue to make laughable money. Even In-N-Out Burger paid people $50 for an interview and $18 an hour. We were making $14 at best. It was perfect for me because I got to wear all my new clothes and laugh at all the phonies who wait at the corner in their Range Rovers and Mercedes (I have both at home) and put on their snobby look. After all, somehow, that makes someone look wealthier, doncha know.

I had to keep my ego in check. It was essential to remember my positions before landing in Orange phony county. I worked for a software company that went public. An investment bank company that brought Starbucks public. At the same time, I sat back and laughed that there wasn't anyone in this country who would purchase a cup of coffee for $2; it just seemed unconscionable. I kicked myself for not getting in from the bottom at $17 per share. After all, Dunkin Donuts was the end-all for coffee drinkers. Several other companies were in my curriculum vitae that would surely impress any corporate mogul to date.

The Trophy Wife

I often wondered if the phonies knew that they were phony. I think all people know who they are unless they came from an effed-up family who distorted their entire image of themselves for the good or bad. That could make for a lonely life. In that, you were so fuggily that your parents told you how beautiful/handsome you were. Maybe you wouldn't be an overachiever. You'd be more of a lazy slob/underachiever waiting for some prince or princess to come to sweep you away. Then there would be some famous book about you like Amelia Havisham in *Great Expectations*, only this time it would be nonfiction. You'd be sitting around for the rest of your pathetic life just waiting for that special someone.

I say this because I have a friend who repeatedly tells her daughter this. I could not wait to meet this beautiful girl, who was so tall, had long beautiful legs, long thick blond hair, the works. She sits home every day at twenty-one, does nothing with her life, doesn't drive due to PTSD from a minor fender bender, and doesn't spend time in school. Mom does nothing except that she goes with her daughter on shopping sprees and doctor's appointments. These doctors' appointments are needed for the imaginary anxiety that has become an addiction to valium. I met this seventh wonder; words cannot explain the horror and shock I felt inside.

On the other hand, mom was just that delusional. She considered herself a "trophy wife" to a man who looks like a fat pig devouring potato chips every night and loves them more than his wife. She's nobody's fool. She stocks the house with everything from

Twinkies, Slim Jims, and any carbohydrate that would clog a young man's heart, a cardiologist's nightmare at age fifteen.

He has money. He wants a divorce every month, but where is Fat man going? He allowed his wife to sit on her ass for twenty-three years of marriage; the only way to do this is in a good detective story. Get rid of the dead weight. Else, Fat man, you are confined to a life of alimony, a studio apartment, and a forced lean diet. Fat man, you have some choices to make. I hadn't seen this woman for a while, but when I did, she was gaunt. Face pale and sucked in, she lost twenty-five pounds and was emaciated. She must have seen the shock on my face and told me she and her family had just recovered from COVID. The problem is, four weeks later, she looked the same.

I said to her, "Are you okay?"

She said, "I think so. I'm going for a colonoscopy tomorrow."

That's the last I saw or heard from her. My immediate thought was Fat man had found a new solution.

On the last day before my vacation, I went in to see a nervous David with Dot standing behind me. I asked him when our next raise would be. He said when the cost of living goes up, usually. This is going to be good.

The Twelve-Month CPI Ended in 2021

Current US inflation rates: 2000–2023

The annual inflation rate for the United States is 6.5 percent for the twelve months ended December 2022 after rising 7.1 percent previously, according to U.S. Labor Department data published January 12. The next inflation update is scheduled for release on February 14, 2023, at 8:30 a.m. ET. It will offer the rate of inflation over the twelve months ended January 2023.

*The latest inflation data (twelve-month based) is always displayed in the chart's final column.

Table: Annual Inflation Rates by Month and Year

Since figures below are twelve-month periods, look to the December column to find inflation rates by calendar year. For example, the rate of inflation in 2021 was 7.0 percent.

The last column, "Ave," shows the average inflation rate for each year *using CPI data*, which was 4.7 percent in 2021. They are published by the BLS but are rarely discussed in news media, taking a back seat to a calendar year's actual rate of inflation.

https://www.usinflationcalculator.com/
The 7 percent increase will be equitable and fair, and I'm sending…

ADVENTURES OF A BOUGIE NEW YORKER

The seven-percent raise will be equitable and fair, and I'm sending "thank you" cards out in advance to prepare for my first day back. After all, it is the polite thing to do. I may have mentioned that my family of origin is a bit, um, let's say, eccentric, but I was taught good manners:

> Never talk with food in your mouth.
>
> No elbows on the table, but wrists are okay.
>
> Take your hat off when you sit down.
>
> Yes, please; no, thank you.
>
> Never go to a home empty-handed.
>
> Do not stab your meat.
>
> May you please pass the butter.
>
> Always wear clean underwear.
>
> If you need to flatulate, go into the bathroom, and use spray (don't blame the dog, people are wise).
>
> Never push an elderly person down the stairs because you're in a hurry.
>
> Don't chew gum like a cow chewing its cud.
>
> Always send a thank you card.

Deanna had sent out an email early in August, followed by a phone call. She asked that all super sweepers attend a two-hour meeting before school started. We would get paid for those two hours. Of course, I'll be there, $28, taxable income. I'm no fool. This is going to be good. They are going to talk about the increases and promotions. How do I handle getting a boost and promotion while maintaining the friendships I've made? There's plenty of truth to the saying "It's lonely at the top." It sure is.

Dot never came back to school. I heard that the disappearance of Connor was all too much for her. Being with her child was more important than the meager wages the sweepers were paid. She didn't need it and needed to keep her child close. Well, she wasn't a child but instead a teen. Who was I to let her in on that? I will never forget Dot and how I could get away with poking fun at her God. She would become so agitated but too Christian to let me have it. That made it even more fun. Did you ever see someone turn red and foam at the corners of their mouth, mutter words, and spin while they piddle away? That was Dot, all right. I'll find another one to pick on. Maybe Funnel. She's too easy. Plus, she's not in work enough to be of some comedic value. She's gone rogue far too often.

I guess it will just be imagining who was getting the added stretch belt and the additional fees on the plane that will keep me occupied for now. Believe me, that'll keep me busy until Christmas vacation.

The Friday before school, I texted Funnel because I was supposed to wait for this critical information about a meeting being held for two hours on Monday. I asked her how she was, and she said she had three seizures, and the doctors thought she might have lost her memory for good.

I told her she'd better not be seizing all over me because my stomach can't handle it, and we don't carry pencils. I also told her that I'd be the one to let her know if she lost her memory. I'm thinking of just gaslighting her. It's always good to tell some good jokes to make yourself laugh.

It was sad going into the room for that meeting. Deanna wasn't holding that meeting as she intended and led us to believe. It was some woman who was a kook. I most certainly didn't like her. I don't like new employees taking old employees' places, especially when they offer no explanations. Deanna's nameplate was still neatly placed at her window. The usurper demonstrated how deviant she could become; she began handing out copies of job descriptions and expectations. I am aghast! Well, if someone isn't going to say something, I am. When will we be getting our increases? I've just met my match.

With eyes flared, she stopped everything, looked up at me, and gave me a cold stare. We both had a staring contest, so to speak. She said sternly, "Well, that's up to the parents."

Say what? Are your six-figure salaries and bonuses up to the parents as well? I thought to myself. Apparently, the usurper will stay until Deanna comes back. I can do this. Indeed, I can.

Meet Judy

I'm going to humanize the usurper and tell you her name. Her name is Judy. Now Judy had her claws wrapped around this job as if her life depended on it. It always reminded me of those creepy *Lifetime* movies where Ellen Burstyn, who would play Judy, would sneak into Doc Robert's apartment and strangle him with a scarf. At the same time, he lay sleeping, which became this homicide case. At the end of these movies, the perp always gets caught, and we find out that she has this mad crush on ole Doc Robert, and she can't bear to live without seeing him every weekday to stalking him on the weekends. She's then handcuffed and sent to the woman's penitentiary. She's made to wear men's boxer shorts instead of that Arizona penitentiary where the men are made to wear pink panties.

And she was bossy. Bossy people are impolite. They say what they mean and mean what they say. Always sounding mean. Everything was an immediate goddamn emergency with Judy. I knew it like I knew the sun came up every morning. Judy wanted this job, and she was here for the taking. She would prove to everyone she was better than Deanna and that she deserved this position. Nobody was going to take her from ole Doc Robert. The verbal orders and panicking modes were so evident to the children. They used to say, "Calm down, Karen!" I had to laugh. How did these young children know about being a "Karen"? Oh, never mind. For a minute there, I had forgotten they were from Orange County, and the moms always say it about each other. The children are just absorbent sponges who regurgitate what is heard.

Meet Karen

Nobody knows where this phrase began for those unclear about a Karen meme. But it's depicted as a specific middle-class white woman whose behavior stems from White privilege. She is the demands to "speak to the manager" type. She belittles their services and threatens to call the police over minor or, in most cases, fabricated stories. Still some argue it emerged from the "speak to the manager" meme as a joke in 2014. Whatever it is, or when it was established, who gives a shite, it is as funny as all hell when you see a kid saying, "Calm down, Karen." You know that kid's got moxie!

Judy made our lives miserable. As if we weren't working hard enough in the August heat, she would tack on these other ridiculous petty things for us to do. For instance, she'd say, "Put up these plastic chains so the children won't go through them when they finish breakfast. They will need to walk around them. Penny, you'll oversee, making sure they walk through that way. And as soon as they leave the area, you can sweep. But don't sweep while they're still eating."

I thought this was a far cry from when we first started working with her. When I went to pick up the broom, she told me, "No, you don't have to do that." Well, that lasted three days. She got used to it real fast. The funny thing about Judy was when one of us tried to reach her on the radio, she would always take it as an emergency and take her stance. Head pointed out, back lowered to get a good starting point, and she would take off running. Like a roadrunner would. What a treat to see this. I mimicked this movement so well that the girls begged me to do it for them plenty of times. I didn't mind; in fact, I liked it. It made me laugh to look like such a goddamn idiot.

Then one day, there was this little boy named Benny. I adored Benny, and if there was ever a little boy, it was him. He was all boy. Snakes and snails and puppy dog tails. He would spend almost all his lunchtime looking for bugs and playing with them. Sometimes, when the music was on, he would dance to the sound of the bass, which was cool because it was *bam*, *bam* with a rugged bad boy walk. Benny was in kindergarten, but he was fantastic. The first day I met him, I thought he was special needs. Benny would look at me, run to the wall, and bang his head against it playfully, like a thingamajikee.

The more I said you can't do that, the more he did it. He even pretended to be getting dizzy. But he wouldn't stop. I radioed Judy and asked her if she could come out to the courts. She said in a little bit. This was the first time I thought she didn't treat this like an emergency. So I made it one.

I told her, "You must come now. I have a boy here banging his head against the wall and will not stop."

She was wise to take on that responsibility. There she was, the roadrunner running our way. Well, Benny took one look at her and ran. He ran from her and then ran some more. It was hilarious! She finally wrapped her would-be talons around the boy and what was said, "I'll never know, but I hope to one day" I must admit, I knew the boy was goofing around, but I wanted to cause undue stress in Judy's life. I wanted to see Karen. I missed her that day. Turns out she was having a meeting with the ole John Robert. I imagined her fluttering her eyelash extensions. I doubt he even noticed.

Another day, a "Gummy Bear" song played on the stream player. The girls and I stood in shock. The entire kindergarten through first grade went mad dog crazy for this song. We couldn't believe what we were seeing. They all gathered on the makeshift dance floor, a concrete block surrounded by the laptop that played the music. There was no room to be had. Not one more space for another child. It spilled out onto the sidewalk into the basketball court. This was not to happen. All the dancing took place in the concrete corner, but there was no control. It was a rave! They were squeezing each other, holding hands, and circling the baseball field where they'd come back, hugging and pressing some more. That's when some boy started to choke. Paula spotted him first and radioed to Funnel, the closest to the boy, to grab the boy in the orange. We didn't want Karen to roadrunner over there or draw panic to anyone else.

Paula ran as fast as she could and quickly told the boy to take deep breaths. He was crying. He got the wind knocked out of him from being squeezed so tightly. Paula took him to the nurse, and that was it. Gawd damn, Judy forbade us from having music anymore. That was a harsh punishment, I thought. After all, music and dancing improved the condition of the heart and lungs, increased muscular strength, better coordination, agility, and flexibility, and Karen wanted to take it all away! Wasn't it enough that these kids were sitting in class with masks on all day long? How about they sat all year long with masks in the classroom and outdoors? And you can't give these children a break, you satanic bitch!

The school was quiet all week long, with no music, hotter than hell. The super sweepers walked around with umbrellas because the sun was just brutal. On Friday, Paula and I decided to say, "F*ck 'em. We're playing the music." And we did. And the school came alive. The children were dancing, the sweepers were dancing, we were all singing a favorite song, and Judy was angry. You could see it in her eyes. We made an executive decision on our own. Too bad, witchee. She would never approach me since the first time she did when she asked if it was an effort for me to get to school on time. I said, "Yes, sometimes." That's honest. I mean, since the disappearance of Deanna.

I often wondered why Judy never told purple paws to wear gloves. She would tear these pints of milk open, put them down, or rip the cellophane off the food like a stray dog and place it on the plate. I wanted to say something, but it was hard to interrupt. "Sit down, or I'll slap you!" Holy crap. None of the sweepers would ever say a word. Hell, we would always protect one another unless we just couldn't.

For instance, these two sisters were continually fighting. Sometimes, it turned into fisticuffs. One was in fifth grade, the other in fourth. I felt like being a smartass one day, and while the fourth grader complained about her sister in front of her, I said, "Well, maybe she doesn't like your home. Maybe she doesn't want to live there. I know lots of foster homes in Compton." Oh, hell no. I did not just say that! I gave them a wink. A smile and everything I could to alleviate the trouble I knew I would get into when these OC brats go to their parents and tell them what the supervisor said. Please, God, let them forget I don't want to sit in front of David to have the discussion again.

Well, as it turned out, it was Paula who was called in. Paula! Yes! The girls told their parents it was Paula, and the mother called in to tell David precisely what was said. I must admit she did get the story mixed up. Mine was much better, but Paula kept her mouth shut and said it wasn't her.

The next day, I saw Paula in the office with David. I said to myself, "Put a fork in me. I'm done."

CA Labor Law Hutzpah, No Bueno

As sure as shit, there's that gawd damn note, "Penny, please see me before you leave." Okay, but what's interesting is that you're not going to pay me for the time I must spend with you. This brings me to the next issue. You'd like me to read your school's emails in my free time at home. Do you realize that California labor laws state that for any work I perform at home, for non-exempt workers, even if it's answering my phone to your fat ass, I get paid for two hours? That's why I never answer the phone, David. That's why I never know what's happening at the elementary school. I don't look at emails after work. If you're not paying me to do so, I don't do it. I don't give away free labor. So call me Norma Rae, I won't be insulted, but I won't see you this afternoon. I will see you tomorrow morning on my clock. I'm not going to remove the note just so I don't rattle your cage more than mine's been rattled. Toot alou.

The following day, I did go to see David. He asked if I saw the note, and I said yes, but I had a commitment and had to leave. I mean, what can you say to that, right? That's why I throw that word around as often as possible; remember that, readers, it works every time, "commitment."

He told me he had gotten a call from an upset mother. Did I say anything to Samantha and Paris about living in foster homes?

"Yes, David, I did. It was said in jest. The two had been arguing and hitting one another at home, and I suggested one of them live outside the home. There was nothing more to it than that."

"Penny, please watch what you say to these children because these mothers quickly call the school and go on a rampage."

"Yes, David, I will. Thank you."

To hell, I will not! These moms are just playing mom because they know they have a reason to act like a mom, between the shopping sprees and the parties and who can outdo whom. And the "Honey, Sadie Crosby just got the brand-new Range Rover 2024 SuperSport Edition. I want 2024 all-equipped bells and whistles with complete carfection! I'd like you to call the dealers from here to Santa Barbara until we find what I want. When we get it, let's not make it obvious to the Crosbys."

And do you know what the kicker is? We have a phony who plays into this wannabe act at school. She gets a Mercedes or BMW every year and acts as if she just bought it. Then she talks to the other super sweepers like she has it like that. That her husband is a doctor, we find out she leases her cars, and her husband is a PA. Phony full of baloney. I'd like to see someone's pants go on fire, watch a nose grow as they move their jaws. Then you'd never have to guess whether these phonies are telling the truth or this is just another phony lie.

It's getting into the cooler weather, and I'm still staring at Deanna's nameplate on her window. I'm beginning to lose hope of her ever coming back. I wrote her texts, "I'm losing the will to live. We miss you," and anything to bait her, but it didn't look good. Judy is staying, and I just know it. That sixth sense tells me it's time to stay or go, Penny. There's no middle-of-the-road here. No negotiations are taking place. I'm walking, watching, thinking, and *bam!* Just like that! I get hit in the side of the head with a goddamn basketball. I feel faint; I fall.

I woke up in Hoag Hospital with the smell of old people. You know the scent; the whiff of a sour stink clogs your nostrils when an ancient relic gets up from a couch, chair, or bus seat. And then you're going to want to throw up in your own mouth? There were the usual smells of Byrex spray and staph infections wafting through the air. Everything seemed blurry, and I had a screaming headache. And to add to the pain I was already feeling, I heard, "Ow, oh, it hurts. No. Somebody help me. Ow, oh, it hurts. I'm dying. This is it…" It was the annoying old fucker next to me. Am I in the Alzheimer's wing? I'm not kidding around here.

Maybe I couldn't remember my name when asked. Perhaps I couldn't even remember it now. Let's see. P-E-N-N-Y. Ha! I remember, and my last name is. OMG, what is my last name? Where is my husband? What's going on? I'm going through the alphabet to figure out my last name. A, B, C, D…it's not happening. I can't get my last name into my correct anterior temporal lobe. I'm done. It's over. I'm sorry, God, for every bad thing I have ever done that I can't remember. I don't want to lose my long-term memory. There's a lot to remember, and I can't recall. Help! Help! Somebody!

Like magic, a nurse came from around the curtain. She told me to please calm down and that she would be with me in a minute. She ran out of the room and returned with a small cup of pills and some water. I said, "What the hell is this? Why are you drugging me? Am I in a mental institution? What's going on here?"

"Mrs. Sloan (*there she said it, said my last name*), these are just to calm you down."

"And why shouldn't I be upset?"

"Mrs. Sloan, you've been involved in a head injury accident. Chances are ninety-five percent that you are experiencing a head concussion, so you aren't sure where you are. If you would just take these, I will go over everything. Please, Mrs. Sloan, I am here to help you. I'm leaving the room now and will be back in five minutes."

That's when I heard it. Another Amber Alert. Only this time, it was different. The news said it was a Caucasian man with two children from Wisconsin. Now they are looking for him in Southern California. Thoughts riveted to the scene with Connor. I remembered the sounds of the helicopters circling around and around until nightfall.

The anxiety and panic had come back. My memory was just fine.

"Nurse! Nurse!"

"Yes, Penny, I'm back."

"I want to see my husband and want to go home now."

"But we'd like to run some tests. We want to make sure there aren't any brain bleeds. You would be leaving against medical advice."

I said that I was fine and I was going home. It was then that I saw the glimmer of my husband's beautiful eyes.

I was given instructions on what to expect with a concussion and a prescription for ibuprofen five hundred milligrams. Just then, my phone rang.

"Hi, Penny. It's John." *John?* "I heard you were injured today on the field. I'm calling to see if everything is okay?"

Oh, I bet you are. I'm sure you also heard I was rushed to the hospital, and you're not sure if my lawyer will be sending papers soon. "Yes, Dr. Robert, I'm leaving the hospital. I'm told I have a concussion and will be out of work for five days. I'm told I shouldn't drive, so I'll see you all when I get back." I felt relieved that I had some time to sort out how I really felt.

I've made my decision. I'm leaving elementary school.

Middle School Blues

I walked into Laguna Beach Middle School and felt like these people were wearing left-wing/liberal masks. The energy was peculiar; nobody complimented me on my outfit. It was my first day. Dammit, why doesn't anybody give a shite? This is supposed to be the Avant-Garde center of Orange County. This is where all the artists present their incredible works of art. Gifting a goddamn compliment may convey that they were less than.

I heard these parents let these obnoxious teens get away with far too much, and I'm here to straighten this mess out. The principal is no Doc Robert, not the savvy, well-dressed, form-fit, masked Robert with veneer teeth. More like a slob with sneakers and an armpit face. I don't think a man in such a leadership position should wear facial hair. It just looks sloppy. My respect is chipping away. He walked right past me like I was a nobody, and he'd seen me here several times before. How rude! I guess it's better that way to get lost in the crowd.

Like when Paula was the first to be pointed out. I still think that's comical. I miss that team. I wondered if Funnel made it through an entire week since I've been gone. I wondered about a lot of things. The girls initially kept me in the loop, but the communication has become less and less. I did hear that Doc Robert was retiring and moving to Texas in January. A friendly Red State. Ever since he gave notice, he's been wearing his cowboy boots. What a racket. I don't think I could hold in my laughter had I been there myself. I wondered if he was sporting a western bolero and suede jacket. Goodbye, Vespa. Giddy up, Stallion.

Overall, the District must have been good to him if he could retire at such a young age. And get this, I don't want to be a teacher. After all, in both schools, I've seen these entitled beings are just too much to bear.

It started on my first day at junior high. This one girl walked past me three times and called me a "bitch" under her breath. What was I to do? It was so sneaky and unassuming that there was nothing I could say or do, and it was always around a group of girls that would have naturally stood up for her. I was appalled. Now usually, I'm the one in charge. Nobody gets away with this, but I'm losing control here and am not happy about it.

The following scenario was to keep these kids on the break line for a snack in an orderly fashion. This blond-haired kid with blue eyes and an overbite walked up to me and said, "Fucker, fucker," to me. Well, I'm going to get him. As sure as shit, I'm going to get that goddamn kid.

We have what is called a mug shot book. It's simply a yearbook that shows every student at the school. If there is a student you don't know, who is uncontrollable, you can hopefully find them in this book. Sometimes, the child has changed so much since the year before that they are hard to recognize, complicating it. But I got him! I got that fucker!

I charged into the assistant principal's office. She was pleasant in the eyes and very endearing. I showed her the picture, and she nodded her head.

She said, "Yes, sometimes, we have trouble with him."

He's spectrum. I wanted to disappear and become invisible. Why didn't I recognize the signs? Especially when he started to call me "Karen, Karen" right after that. And then the little girl standing behind him said he made her cry every day. "He calls me a Nazi."

This explains it all. What a fool I am. I apologized and quickly left the room.

I remember back when the only thing that embarrassed me more was when I ran for the train one morning and forgot to pull my dress over my pantyhose. It was the middle of rush hour. A courageous woman came to me and whispered, "Your dress is up." It took me a few seconds to decipher what she was telling me and then a few seconds more to catch my breath because I felt I was going to faint. Do you know that feeling when you get a hot rush pulsing on your face? Well, I had it. At that time, they had ventilated panties. For the first time in all my years of travel, I began seeing the same people every day, on the same train, at the same time year after year. To this day, I shudder to think about my degrading experience. I don't wear pantyhose anymore, but I do wear panties.

This new boy, Aaron, became my Connor. He held my heart. We even had nicknames for one another. He'd call me Vegan, and I'd call him Vegan back. He had an overbite with a space between his teeth. You could use a tree limb to floss them, but it gave him character, I thought to myself. Let's face it, the kid's got chutzpah! He also had a paraprofessional called "Cool Guy" because nobody knew his name, and he had that cool guy look. Dark hair, ponytail, dark glasses, worn jeans, and black boots.

One day, it was comical because he was wearing a light blue shirt with black jeans, and Aaron was wearing light blue shorts with a black T-shirt. Aaron had Cool Guy wrapped around his finger. He would walk out of class and down the stairs, and Cool Guy would take two steps simultaneously to keep up with him. Aaron could ditch you in a NY minute. Just like that, without saying a word, he'd just walk into the boy's room, and Cool Guy would be left looking side to side, front and back. It was such a game Aaron played, and I enjoyed watching it. The more I paid attention to Aaron, the more shy he became. I missed the ornery kid Aaron once was to me. Now when I wave, he waves back. When I smile, he smiles back. That's not how I wanted it to be. I miss the fucker.

He was so brilliant in an Elon Musk sort of way that he had said something to Cool Guy that could have destroyed his entire career. Possibly life. The school couldn't have that, so I guess ole Aaron needed a higher level of care. I miss him. Rumor has it he may be coming back. At least his parents are fighting for it. But it could just be a rumor. You never know what's real or what's not here. It's like swallowing the red pill in the *Matrix.*

When I began working at the junior high school, I wasn't handed a broom or a fluorescent vest, making me feel like a human being and less like a common criminal. These kids are hard to handle. They are the real entitled bitches and bastards of OC. Some of these kids are allowed to just walk around the campus, and we are to look for them and yet not give them a hard time because they are "high priority." You'd think "high priority" would mean someone important, right? Well, they are if you think their parents will prosecute the school. And yet, as they are giving the school employees a hellacious time, the district still wants their asses in their seats come attendance because that's how the school makes its money. Well done. *Clap, clap, clap*. Throw down the mic!

Devil's Spawn

I've seen the movies *The Exorcist* and *The Omen* before, and now I can tell when a child looks possessed. There are two of them in the school, fraternal twins. Here's the rub; these are the kids you are pleasant to, but you never let your guard down because they lack any human emotion, but what they do have is a double dose of cruelty. We have all heard at one time or another that "the devil wears many disguises." These demon spawns have their pack of sheep they run with. They are the shepherds, and these idolaters are their sheep; they will walk off a cliff if led.

The female spawn, Delilah, didn't take to me right from the start. She made snide remarks in the gym dressing room while I was in the office. She knew I couldn't hear, but her snarl and stare said it all. The girls she was with just laughed. She was the only one not laughing, just staring me down. From that moment on, I knew I had made an enemy. I didn't know why, but it gave me the shitters.

Johnny, the male spawn, was kinder to me but would not listen or give in to any rules. Rules did not apply to him. Anything we said was just wasted breath. We also knew he was going into the boy's bathroom almost daily, graffitiing the walls, yet we could never catch him in the act.

When one of us would yell, "Supervisor! Is anyone in here?" he'd say, "Yeah, it's Johnny, and I'm dropping a deuce!"

The supervisors had to ensure that nothing was happening in the restrooms. Our responsibility was to ensure that nothing unlawful was going on in there and that nobody hid from class. One male supervisor held Johnny accountable for going to class, and Johnny didn't like it. He was going to get back at the supervisor, all right.

He began to speak loudly and said, "You make me feel uncomfortable. You are standing in the doorway, staring at me. This is illegal. You are a pedophile!"

This was a very calculated attempt to ruin somebody's life. Thank goodness nothing ever came of it. But that goddamn kid could have put somebody in jail and given him a record for life. How do you tell your wife, researching neighborhood pedophiles in the area, just how you made it on the list? Hanging out in the doorway of a schoolboy's bathroom? Weird.

Delilah came sniffing around like a dog about a week later, circling me. I wasn't sure what she was up to, but one of her friends said to me, "So where'd you have the plastic surgery?"

"Excuse me?"

"Plastic surgery, where'd you have it done?"

"Well, let's see. If you were married to a doctor, you could have anything you wanted."

"Wait, you're married to a doctor?"

I sashayed away. Man, did that feel good!

The truth is, I'm not married to a doctor. I'm a trust fund baby. But the one thing I'm not is a goddamn phony. I guess that sounds like an oxymoron, and it is, but nobody needs to know my business. But I love to know theirs. And this is the reason for writing this book. You readers need to know theirs too.

ADVENTURES OF A BOUGIE NEW YORKER

You get as much respect as flipping hamburgers, being a student supervisor in Orange County. This is until you are handing out campus cleanup slips. Then it becomes a serious issue, and now you are in charge. Campus cleanup punishment doesn't allow for girlfriend/boyfriend time. It's a goddamn burden on these kids, and I love it every time I write one. Now don't get me wrong, I don't arbitrarily write them to write them.

I give these kids wide births a lot of the time, but when they think they've outsmarted me, the Scorpio in me comes out. I do believe there's something to horoscopes.

As it turned out, I must have given the "wrong kid" a slip because I was standing in the lunch area at lunchtime, which is only thirty minutes of sheer hell of who can break lines and get their food first and scarf it down in time for class. When once again, *bam!* I got hit in the head with goddamn chocolate milk on the same side as the basketball. This time it was intentional. Chocolate milk sprayed all over my hair and my expensive outfit. I was embarrassed, and I was mad as hell! I didn't show it. I wiped my hair and slowly walked away toward the office.

I was searching for the assistant principal, the principal, or the office manager. No one was around. I wanted to look at the videotapes in the area where they targeted me to see what rat bastard did it. I wanted expulsion immediately! "High priority" can kiss my ass when someone comes close to losing my eye.

Finally, the principal called my name on the radio, and we looked at the tape together. The video was so illegible that it looked like the trial drone footage the prosecution gave in the Rittenhouse trial that was a travesty of justice.

Nobody, I mean nobody, could be made out in the school's tape. Just a group of silhouettes. I wasn't going to give up; this was just another parody of events in a school supervisor's life.

I loathed the position more each and every day I was there.

That following Monday, I made sure my first stops were the principal's office, the assistant principal's office, and the office manager's office. I was not going to let this go. I was also going to ensure this was never going to happen again. As suspected, nobody had answers for me. I felt insignificant, belittled, and disrespected. That same afternoon, the principal and the assistant principal made their presence known in that same area where the brutality happened. That was the last time I was sentenced to that post.

I was sitting outside the bathrooms just yesterday, and Johnny was in the boy's bathroom for quite a long time. This was not unusual, although we usually think he is graffitiing or some other form of delinquency. But instead, I caught this sweet smell of vape aroma from the boy's bathroom. I knocked on the door and said, "Supervisor coming in." I saw those black kicks in the last stall. Likened to the ones worn by the thirty-nine cult members waiting for the Hale-Bopp. The room was emanating vape smoke.

"Johnny, is that you in the last stall?"

"What is it with your supervisors coming into the bathroom!"

"Johnny, I smell vape."

"So. It's like a cop wanting to search your car illegally. The Fourth Amendment protection against unlawful search and seizure makes police car searches illegal."

"Johnny, who was in here before you?"

"How the hell should I know?"

The best defense is a good offense, which this is a prime example. This kid would make a perfect defense or prosecuting attorney.

I have heard him mention the law one too many times. He's like a goddamn mini-Johnny Cochran.

I began to realize everything was a tug-of-war with these kids. At least ten percent of them. It was mentally exhausting. It wasn't worth it. Between the parents and their kids and listening to the stories of the districts whining that they don't have enough money, not enough money? These school districts have tons of money. The school unions are the richest in the country. It's a goddamn lie, just like when Joe Biden opens his mouth. It's a blatant prevarication.

Although just for the hell of it, I would like a glimpse at that "bad dude, Cornpop." And why is it that just because you don't like Biden makes you a Trumpster? That's the problem in this country. It's either or. You're either for Trump or for Biden. Period. You can hate politics, but you're taught to hate the men themselves.

I have lived many years, but not enough to have ever seen this. Will we ever come back from this division, for fucks sake? People say Trump started it, but did it start when Hillary lost? Was it Trump's ego? Is it the onset of Joe's dementia or the behind-the-scenes control in Joe's administration? One day, the truth will come out, and perhaps we will all be shocked, or maybe we won't. Maybe this is all practice to answer to the Chinese Communists down the line. Their one-hundred-year plan could be on year 95 as of now. One must feel the madness surrounding us. Freedoms and liberties are being taken away until it begins to feel normal. Was George Orwell a visionary after all?

Will the babies born today never learn the history I knew because of this new "Woke" generation? Shall I sell my copy of *If I Ran the Zoo* for up to a thousand dollars like the others I see? How about *McElligot's Pool* for a few hundred dollars. These vintage books were taken off the shelves because they depicted cultural differences by obvious physical differences. I am Irish. Suppose the Irish were to demand that every book depicting an Irish person with unruly red frizzy hair, pale skin, an upturned nose, and freckles be banned. In that case, somehow, I don't think it could be pulled off. This cancel culture needs to grow some thick skin. No one in this world will hurt the feelings that will brilliantly depict me. I had hoped Dr. Seuss would have never wanted to cause any hurtful subliminal messages. Shall I listen to angry music like rap so I can be in the "in" crowd? I thank Jaysus for having a husband who shares a generation with me that we like the same music and appreciate the same bands.

How could I go out with an old fucker who doesn't even know who *Third Eye Blind* is? It's not even a given today until you start humming "Doo, doo, doo, doo-doo-doo-doo," and then it's, oh yeah, I know that band. This isn't even a song that I would suggest listening to because that's a simple pop song. Stephan Jenkins is a lyrical genius and not a '90s pop band, as people have retorted. Man, that makes my blood boil. But you can't say that with that goddamn angry rap noise drowning out your eardrums, feeling like you want to go out and reenact the film *The Purge*.

It's Wednesday, and, as usual, I see Delilah in the first-period PE class. She never participates in class because she tells me it's unimportant and that "no matter what, they are going to pass me along to seventh grade anyway. They must."

"Delilah, you'd better rethink this and do well in high school. You need to get into a good college."

"I'm not going to college."

"Why not?"

"It costs too much money."

"Delilah, no, it doesn't. You take out loans, and when you graduate, you land a good job and can begin to pay those loans back."

"Penny, why do all the boys in this school think you're ugly?"

Gulp.

"I mean, why does everyone hate you so much? I tell them to be nice to you, but—"

"I don't know, Delilah. They think Ms. Carole is beautiful."

"Well, Ms. Carole is beautiful!"

Well, if you think a milky-skinned woman in her late '60s with body fat is beautiful, so be it! And I'll tell you another thing, that smile she wears is built on sarcasm. Don't let it fool you. You're one in the same spawn, child.

We are short on supervisors, so the students are wild. We have the runners who disappear off campus and the vapors in the bathrooms who deny they were standing on the toilet seats vaping. Yet we are walking into a cloud of smoke. Last Friday was the dance, and Delilah and a friend were running around campus, screaming, "Fuck you!" to the teachers. But there they were, at school on Monday. I can't make this stuff up. But fortunately, there's always a Dick to hire.

Meet Mark

Mark was hired, and we are all relieved because he came from a High School and is pleasant and friendly. He's really outgoing and a pleasure to be around. I now call him Dick. Dick decides to be a hotshot and tells the principal, Peter, that everyone wears a vest at the high school. Hence, the students always see the supervisors coming. What a goddamn genius. We are now relegated to wearing extra-large neon orange mesh vests. He is the annihilator. I have never committed a felonious act in my lifetime. Yet I am demoted to looking as if I pick up trash on the side of the highway.

I wanted to scream, "In thirty goddamn years, this school has never required the supervisors to wear vests, and now Dick brings it up, and it's a great idea?" We are allowed to use markers to write our names on the vest so that the student can say, "Well, the supervisor said I could do this." And that's our cue: "Oh yeah, which supervisor?" What a bunch of doozies. I've returned in time and concluded that every workplace has a Dick. It's just that ours happens to be named Mark.

Teachers see me wearing this drape of neon shit, saying, "What? With your beautiful clothes? I'll help you write a list of why you shouldn't have to wear that vest." My clothes are too important to that school. Why are they making it so hard on people? It's disgraceful. They should honestly be ashamed of themselves. I give people excitement and beautiful artwork to study every workday. I am a fashionista, and to take that away to wear a piece of shit is just giving people a bad day. I hope you're happy, Ralph Kramden. Now you can pull your "Ralphie Boy" head out of the principal's ass. Because you have a big mouth!

Serial Killer in Training

But I'll tell you what, there are phonies at other levels in work too. For instance, the custodian. When it comes to long yellow rubber duck raincoats, all the supervisors are sure to have one. Everyone apart from me. Even people hired after I have one. When I asked why I didn't have one, the custodian answered, "We don't have none left. I can ask if we can order some, but I don't know." So you're telling me brain shit that you secretly walked around, gave everyone a raincoat, and left me out that same day. There were torrential downpours, cold rain, and wind. I had a short winter jacket and wet jeans, and you taunted me by asking me where my raincoat was. You never mentioned that you had two extras because you saved them for the afternoon male staff. Since we are so secretive, how about I secretly call the communists and notify them where you are? Quid pro quo?

I don't like people like this. These are the people you can't trust at work. They are untrustworthy. The trim rat packers are saving their stash for their favorites. Be off, little man; they call you on the radio because a dog pooped on the stairs and a dead bird is sliced open on the grass. I'm wondering if the male spawn did it.

I take that back. It wasn't too long after that that the custodian approached Ms. Carole and me and shook a garbage bag. We heard scratching but didn't know what to think. The wanker had a live mouse caught in a mouse trap, smiling ear to ear. I am an animal activist and found this very disturbing and telltale of a human being's character. I concluded with the question of who sliced that bird.

This is the last week of school before recess. Gifts are being handed out to most teachers and their students, office workers to other workers, etc. I wanted to give the office workers something pretty to put on their desks, so I brought in eight poinsettias for each lady a week before. I was so proud of myself. How wonderful and thoughtful I am. To think of these ladies that I hardly know but probably don't get much recognition. I am the best.

That afternoon, I noted that the poinsettias I had given the assistant principal were placed outside, still wrapped in plastic on a table. It was cold and not much sunlight that afternoon. I thought it odd and rude. On the last day before vacation, I heard my teammate, who was given the long yellow rubber coat, overly thanking the assistant principal for something. Hmmm. Now I know she left a two-dollar mega-million ticket in our mailbox. (Brother, can you spare a dime?) To go on and on with such redundancy, thanking her like that, could not have been over a two-dollar mega-million ticket. Again, I'm made to feel like an imposter, left in the dark. I purposely left my mega million ticket in my mailbox. That's where it will stay until the dust collects for the new supervisor's start date. Reminding myself that nobody wants this job.

This is an unfortunate group of leaders. They have offered these open positions to several people, and nobody will take them. They will have one more opening to fill; mine, because you need to walk when you feel unappreciated. I told you earlier in this book that I didn't need the job; I certainly don't want this treatment.

The surprising thing is that I thought Laguna Beach was going to be different. In a good way. I discovered that it was snootier and cattier than the school I had just left. Just a big bunch of phonies. I miss Newport.

I've been told that three groups of cartel children attend the school. I don't know who they are, but I don't want to step on anyone's toes. I don't need the headaches. They don't cause trouble and keep to themselves in their small groups.

Within the first two months I was there, I saw police cars and sheriffs with some Mexican students sitting at tables. I was petrified because I didn't expect to see what I saw, and I don't like to be around so many guns in plain sight. I was so nervous for the other students to see this that I asked them to go through the staff office so they didn't have to be privy to what was happening. My teammate asked me why I did that, and I said I didn't want them exposed to that. She said, "Why not?" as if we were at a petting zoo or something.

She said, "You shouldn't have told them to do that."

I asked what was going on there.

She said, "It's probably some gang-related stuff or something." So casually, I might add. I'm sorry, but I'm not up for Columbine bullshit today. I need to get home on time and walk my Labradoodle, besides which she needs a change of clothes. The dog park just gets a kick over her wardrobe. Sometimes we dress alike. I have my unique tailor who whips up some funky clothing for us. They would be disappointed if I didn't show.

Here's where it gets funny. The Armpit rarely makes a showing. When he does, he pretends he's never seen my face before, and because of that, I wondered if that were true; why didn't Armpit ask who I was and why I was on campus grounds? What a goddamn phony. So many times I needed him to step in and give me direction. He just redirected me to the assistant principal with soft eyes. He just didn't give a good goddamn about the kids or the underpaid detectives. He was there to collect his paycheck to buy cheap clothes. The staff barely answered when I asked them, "What does he do?" Their retort was a muttered, "He deals with district stuff." All-day? For forty-eight weeks? You knew he was a liberal at that, and if you could tolerate it, so be it. But if not, don't dare look next to his office where the fecking Prius is parked. I bet he just moved here from San Francisco because he couldn't stand the city he helped destroy. Now he wants to ruin Laguna. Begone, you dirty, filthy animal. Go bring filth and sovereignty tide to another town, you circus clown. We have laws here that we like to protect and uphold.

Every school has mean girls. But these mean girls were only mean to me, so it seemed. They would laugh in my face when I asked where they were heading off to. They would reply to me with "It's none of your business." They said my lips were too big, anything they thought would hurt me or get under my skin. But remember, these girls were "high priority." These were the girls that the sheriff made special trips to the school with taxpayers' money just to talk to them and tell them horrible stories of what could happen to them. And that they should never leave the campus unattended during school hours. All the while, a person in need could have used a sheriff at that time of day for an actual true crime. Still these bippies are too self-centered to even think of that. I imagine their parents are too. And just like karmic retribution, it happens. They were the ones in the big houses by the beach. The privileged kids. Not the ones who had the mom who shared a home and had six kids and another on the way. I counted her stimulus checks for lack of anything better to do one day. Holy, that woman made out. What a racket in a Bernie Sanders world. This woman's kids go to school and are well-behaved.

My heart goes out to them because they aren't the ones with the electric bikes or the new skips, but they are very polite, beautiful, and clean. But then there is this shit for brain's priority parent.

Who would make a "Karen" of themselves and demand to see Armpit, who would ultimately send Karen to the assistant principal because he was busy with the district?

"What did that mean, Supervisor, say to my baby?" (Okay, maybe I'm exaggerating, but still.) "Oh no, not my baby. She wouldn't do a thing like that." *Nope, not her. She is too busy being groped or is groping her boyfriend at the lunch tables in full view of the other students.* The mother doesn't even know about the boyfriend. Boy, oh boy, would I love to tell her. There are just so many things…

The only crucial thing is that the student is expected to be in their seat no matter how bad their disposition is. So by now, you understand why being expelled is so rare when it is so needed. Because of the "Every Child Succeeds Act," these children no longer fear failure. They are in the "no matter what" club. This alone puts a lot of pressure on the teachers. While I went to school to be an elementary school teacher, I would pursue my education in teaching alone, as you may have read earlier. After working in junior high, I would never or could never be around kids like these again. I could not have withstood the pressure from what the local, state, and federal guidelines wanted of me when the child just didn't. It's all about the money. But what isn't?

Here's the skinny, working for a school district is quite comical. They are always screaming poverty but are sitting on piles of unused cash from the COVID payouts alone. If you ask for masks for the children, even though the masks are mandated, you get a "make sure the kids know they have to bring them from home; the school can't afford to keep supplying them." Or, for instance, like me. When I did them a favor by staying an extra 3.5 hours, and they had a tizzy fit because their left hand and right hand didn't communicate, they screamed they couldn't afford to pay me that extra half hour. To take it during work. Now I'm going to let you in on a little secret that some of you may not know. The school teachers union is the richest and most powerful in the country. "Knowledge itself is power" (Meditationes Sacrae 1597).

Two days before my departure, a student walked up to my grill without expression and asked if I could move my face. I thought for a moment and immediately wanted to say, "Why no guy, not since that goddamn fastball hit it. Is it that obvious, and are you asking out of concern?" Instead, I said, "Why would you ask me something like that?"

She said, "I don't know," all the while with a straight face. I just didn't know what to say. I know I am more beautiful than these teenage sons of bitches, but why would they pick on me like this? I told her to come with me. I sat her down to write her up.

I asked her name, and she said it was Lucas. I almost dropped my pen!

"Lucas, what grade are you in?" Now you know I'm entirely baffled by "Lucas" because I'd sworn I must've misheard it, and it was "Lucinda" or something.

He smart-ass answered me and said, "Sixth. This is sixth-grade lunch."

I knew that, but again, I was in shock. I said, "Come with me." I took him to the assistant principal and told her what she had told me. He got a "never say anything like that to a lady." That was that.

The assistant principal told me I needed to be careful about addressing him. I said I couldn't help it. He has better skin than me. All the while, I was thinking, why the hell should I be watching what I said when he wasn't even correcting me? He is so confused that he doesn't even know how to answer, and I look as if I'm wrong. What's wrong with this country? He should apologize for screwing up my head and having my boss talk to me about his lack of decision-making. What the...

The following day, word had it that he was genderqueer, aka nonbinary. To tell you the truth, I don't care what you want to call yourself. Just treat me with dignity and respect, and I will do the same. It's no wonder the kid never corrected me. The assistant principal had a stick up her ass, while Lucas didn't care. All these deep dark secrets. "What doesn't come out in the wash will come out in the rinse," my mama always used to say, and there you have it. This kid is a priority kid too.

I have a lot of gay friends in my life. We don't have issues, or shall I say, they don't have problems. They are comfortable with themselves and have a lot of fun. And I have never met people who are so popular in my life. They have no points to prove or people to prove them to. They are happy, joyous, and free. They are blessed and deserving of my love and have given so much love in return. I am blessed as well.

I've realized, all on my own, that there isn't one student supervisor in Orange County that is more beautiful than me. That may sound not quite right to some because we have been taught by religion, society, and whomever to be humble. For cripes sake, Jaysus, who do you think you are? But that's the whole point, isn't it? That we are God's children, and we were made to shine. God made us perfect and did not want society to change us into anything else. Well, I'm doing just that. I'm not allowing any of the Armpits or students in this world to make me break. I can honestly and openly say that those two girls were the most horrible fourteen-year-olds I have ever encountered. I hope to never cross paths with them again.

But truth be told, they are not Connor. God bless his soul. My heart still cries out for him. I try to push the memory out of my head so my heart won't hurt so badly.

But every damn time I see that fiery orange hair on a boy, the pain, the fecking physical pain, comes back and pierces my belly so hard that the water starts trickling from my eyes. It's almost magical how it happens spontaneously like that. It's frustrating how you would give anything to get those three seconds back in time. How I would bargain with God for those three seconds just in time for my Connor to know what I know now, to ensure his safety. He'd be home right now. I would have given him his Valentine's lollipop already. It's a big red heart, with a frosted white top. I've carried the same lollipop in my coat since Connor's disappearance. It's become my talisman.

I started to put my feelers out. I asked around if Newport needed another student supervisor.

It was there that I felt the most needed and cared for. The kiddos were still too young to know evil. At least, that was my take.

As it turned out, Paula called me one night and was excited to tell me there was an opening and that I should return. And that Judy was gone. Gone for good. Yippee, I shouted! And that everyone liked me there. Well, of course, they did. I never did anything egregious toward them; it was an extraordinary time. We all shared a special bond. One that will always remain in my heart. While thinking about how I would return to the kinders, I was rubbing something subconsciously. I outlined the Valentine's Day lollipop of Connors with my pointer finger. I still had hope. Where there is life, there is hope, and where there is hope, life is worth living to your most entire, in the most magnificent way. And douse that happiness onto others, which creates the rippled effect.

ADVENTURES OF A BOUGIE NEW YORKER

I don't mean to get sappy; generally, I'm not a booger and snot type of gal, but when I think about what's ahead for me, it makes me feel all oogly inside, especially leaving that goddamn phony Armpit. The Armpit constantly rolls his eyeballs when he sees me, as if he is so under pressure. I'll tell you what, I'd like to spend one day in his office like a fly on the wall to see what the phony thinks he adds to the district. Bumpkins. That's what. Bumpkins! They were there before him, and they will be there after him. Mr. Self-Important Armpit.

Let's see. You, my assistant, will handle the entire middle school with those scathing, nasty, chip-on-their-shoulder kids while I deal with the district. Jaysus, what is he really dealing with? How many rolls of toilet paper will they order in the year 2023? Will it be the two-ply this year instead of the three-ply? That would save the district gobs of money. How many rolls of paper towels will suffice for the posing janitor, aka practicing serial killer, to do his job efficiently with less paper? Does anybody notice how much they are diluting the cleansers to date? Were these your decisions this year, all year? You're an eegit!

I want to apologize to myself. What I learned is that I was depressed at Laguna. The kids were unruly. I would ask them where they are going. They would answer, "It's nunya your business." This did not hurt my feelings; it angered me. Perhaps that's making light of it. It infuriated me. They would repeat it and walk off the campus, and what was I to do? Be the enforcer. Count to ten and take off like Judy, the roadrunner. Hut, tackle, down, handcuff, and then walk them to the bench outside the assistant principal's office until she gets back from whatever took her away from her post in the first place. And the only thing these girls asked for was their device to show pictures from Frankie's party Friday night.

My husband pleaded with me night after night to quit the asylum, but I'm not a quitter. I'll be damned if I'll let those little bastids win. But they ARE winning because they are renting space in my head.

On the last day at the school, my final straw was that I took that dayglo vest off, handed it to the assistant principal, and said, "Here you go, there's someone out there who needs this job more than me." Now you might be asking yourself, "Why would I apologize to myself?" The answer is simple. Why would I stay in a place that bullied me and made me feel bad for $17 an hour or even $1,700 an hour, especially when I didn't have to? Not because I'm a trust fund baby but because it's about self-love and caring for myself. And when that innermost voice inside me is screaming "leave," I love myself enough to walk, and I chose not to for so long. I was my worst enemy. When did it become okay for anyone to bully me and for me to be okay with it? It is as simple as this: Penny, either let go or be dragged.

I called Westport Elementary and spoke to Annmarie in human resources. I told her I was interested in coming back, and she was happy to hear it. I gave myself a couple of months off to enjoy myself, read, relax, spend time with my dog, and fly to New York for a few weeks. It was heaven.

While in New York, I had dinner at Le Cirque with a longtime friend, Colleen. We talked about all the fun times we had when we were kids and how lucky we were that we didn't grow up in this generation. The waiter stood at the table, and I said, "Yes, sir, here is my vaccination card." We showed him our cards and took off our masks.

Walt Disney

Disney has now gone overboard with this woke stuff. Shit, I'm awake. Are you awake? People, nobody is sleeping. It is so much in our faces that you can't even snooze. Wokers have ruined my planned vacation with my nephew, niece, great niece, and great nephew. Why can't they just leave things alone? Now I must boycott them. No more addressing the patrons with "Welcome, ladies and gentlemen, boys and girls!" Disney always seemed to be about children and families. The family unit. For feck's sake, we were all trapped in a woman's body. We came from our mother's wombs. LGBTQAI+WTF. Now think about that.

Confused? I can't wait until the day scientists pour hot water on ole Walt to revive him. Eventually, he will go out of the cryogenically frozen block he was immersed in and back on the streets. I even bet his clothes will be in fashion once again. I can't wait to see his face when he realizes how wokey his company's gone.

And most importantly, how he's got to stop being a goddamn White supremacist, they will tell him. They'd better keep the liquid nitrogen and oxygen within arm's reach. Ole Walt may want to be submerged back into subzero-degree temperatures. It ain't pretty out there, and it may be too much to bear.

Sometimes, it is, for all of us. I don't care who you are or what you stand for. It's a lot. And if you're self-centered enough to feel the havoc that either you or someone around you is creating, your family is feeling it too. It's the trickle-down system. No one is unscathed or walks away untouched, metaphorically speaking. Disney has lost all its tax deductions, special status, special privileges in Orlando, Florida, and $60 million in market share. They will now pay $360 million in taxes, which they wouldn't have paid before. They should not have pushed the agenda. They didn't live and let live. And I can't think of anything worse in business than losing Johnny Depp. What rational business-minded person allows Johnny to walk away? Do they realize I started watching him in *21 Jump Street* and he has been my heartthrob ever since? *Pirates of the Caribbean* will be a box office failure. And don't let it surprise you if they put a nonbinary actor in there. That would fit right into the agenda. They got rid of Peter Pan and will now introduce *Jamie of the Caribbean* to the pirate screen an androgynous name.

And I'm going to repeat it. I am an Independent. I voted for Obama twice and, dare I say it, Trump once. But what I am is a rationale. I can't be beholden to one party or another because if you were to ask me, I'd tell you, you were insane for asking me, that the world has gone mad. That everyone has an agenda in Congress and whose plan is worse. Who gets the most prominent house in the end? Winna woke chicken dinna.

ADVENTURES OF A BOUGIE NEW YORKER

I was watching a documentary the other night. If I wasn't confused before, I'm confused now. There are approximately nine million American LGBT, included are seven hundred thousand transgenders. Now I don't know about any of you, but my memory is right about shot at this stage. How the hell am I not going to offend someone? I might as well stay indoors; it's safer for me and the rest of the country. Who the hell needs their city set on fire, or my hair scorched, or worse yet, that nasty gray dust on your mug all because you called someone the wrong pronoun? Oh, pishposh! I'll just be on my way now. Do you want to really shit your pants? I'm going to give them to you. But it's up to you to find the definitions of each because they are way long to write. Here goes:

1. Straight
2. Lesbian
3. Gay
4. Bisexual
5. Pansexual
6. Polysexual
7. Asexual
8. Demisexual
9. Gray sexual
10. Queer
11. Autosexual
12. Androsexual
13. Gynosexual
14. Homoflexible
15. Heteroflexible
16. Non-Binary

That's all I know for now, but I'm sure more will be revealed. And all these nouns have some form of meaning or feeling attached to them. It used to be gay, lesbian, or homosexual in my generation. That was it, and it was easy. None of which ever bothered me then and doesn't today.

But again, it was easy to remember. Now as I said, I saw this documentary, and this woman said there are times that she wakes up and can feel like a man, a woman, or even a cat on any given day. I get the man or woman. But what do you do in the last scenario? Go to work, purring and cozying up to people, jumping on their desks, and tasting their tuna. How do you manage that? Do you call into work and say I'm sorry, but I'm feeling like a cat today, and I won't be coming in. Are there personal days set aside for this? I'd like to understand these issues in more depth.

Drugs No Can Do

The United States has been thrown into this bubbling cauldron. We have not been given any instructions on working within its walls. It's unfair to any of us; this is where intolerance begins. Even so, it all adds up to two percent of our population. So why all the whoa? It's only one day at a time we need to get through. Tomorrow hasn't come, and yesterday is over. Stay in the present (today). You will feel a calming sensation if you don't think about a horrible tomorrow or how next year will be if it's anything like last year, only worse.

Personally, it doesn't affect me either way. If you are a law-abiding citizen and you love the United States and want to live here peacefully with the rest of the like-minded people, then so be it; let us all live in peace and harmony. That means teaching Mathematics, Science, History, English, Physical Education, Art and Music. That's your place. Leave the rest to the parents. Stay in your lane. Let children be children. They don't have to grow up so fast. A future is waiting for them, and right now, it doesn't look so pretty. There's time for everything. Let nature take its course. It will; don't rush it.

I love the idea of a uniform for school. Every child and teen wears the same thing. There are no haves and have-nots. Nobody is left out feeling less than others. Kids are not bullied because they are poor or don't have the most fabulous clothes or wear the sexiest outfits. What I saw in middle school left nothing to the imagination. It was an utter disgrace. Yes, there was a dress code. Was it enforced? Never. Armpit was, you know, busy with the district. At the same time, the Assistant Principal had all that discipline to dole out and the Sheriff's to greet. But I can't help but think that during this visit with the sheriff, there could have been several strung-out drug addicts who, at that moment, were stealing an innocent civilian's catalytic converter. This can be ill-gotten right in front of the owner's home. A less than two-minute job is easily worth $50 to $250 to an unscrupulous recycling facility. The precious metals industry is such a hot commodity today. Drug abuse is our primary source of robberies.

It's just like that. The following day, you're cursing the gas tanks in the "Build Back Better" era or your battery operating on your way to work. I see more and more Teslas on the road and Congress talking as if you can just go out and buy one today in a recession. But there's one catch: electricity is rising, and battery charging will soon cost a lot of money. I guess people haven't given much thought between the loans on the Teslas and the electricity charges, and what's more, the lack of Battery Powering Stations around amongst other things. What color is the administration's sky in their world?

You find out on the radio that Trudeau has gone tripolar again and is taking the right to bear arms away from his citizens. But in turn, he is legalizing fentanyl and amphetamines, which makes it okay. He giveth, and he taketh away.

California has become the exodus. Outside of Hawaii, it's the most expensive place to live. Ridiculously expensive. People complain about paying $5 in gas in other states and are mad. Well, news just in, we are paying $6.15 for regular. What a hoot! They even have a website up, "Leaving California." How excited these people are but have observed that their new neighbors are not too happy to have Californians as neighbors; something about fruit and nuts. I don't know; I'm from the east coast. Must be something to it. I don't understand why every seat is taken in the schools. Are they leaving their children behind? Hmmm.

Just as I'm leaving Laguna Hill School for good, who comes walking up the stairwell, none other than Aaron holding both his mom's and dad's hand. I'm assuming they have a meeting with a board member and Armpit. It's been months since I've seen Aaron, and I was so happy to see him. He wore that devilish grin I always liked. He broke loose from Mom and Dad's hands and ran up to me. This was very unusual because he only called me names from a distance. He never came that close. I was somewhat shocked and looked at his parents to see their reactions. They didn't seem rattled, so I went along with it. Whatever "it" was. Aaron came up to me and wrapped his arms around me. He whispered to me, "Come here," so I bent down to greet him. All I heard was "fucker," and he laughed and ran away. Yup, that's Aaron for you. God bless his soul. I hope he never changes.

Here I go; I parked my car and took a few deep breaths; I remembered to read my meditations this morning which always start my day on the right foot. I wore my fabulous Free People two-piece jumpsuit. It's really cool. It's held together by one piece of fabric that makes it a jumpsuit. You can see some of my tummy, but that's okay. I'm in great shape. The truth is the truth.

It was my first day back at Westport Elementary School. I'm a bit frightened because I've never been one to lie or stretch the truth, and here I am with the old crew, trying not to bring up why I had to leave the middle school. Because the principal had a face like an Armpit? That's malicious sounding, but it's not just the Armpit; it's the entire guise. The attitude, the Prius station wagon, the stay in the office and don't come out. If someone interrupts, like me, because I have chocolate milk pouring down the left side of my head, you give me the five-minute sign and point to the phone. To hell, I'll wait! I know, I know, it's the district. You're instrumental in all the planning and Woke bullshit and regulating who needs the COVID test on Mondays. Or did you delegate that to the Assistant Principal as well?

I wanted to tell my team that the kids at the middle school were gnarly, nasty, had no manners, and disrespected any authority figure. Those moms stood next to them like soldiers at Guantanamo Bay. But what good would that do me? I would only tell them if they even thought about working there. I'd have to spare them from the emotional pain and PTSD. Save them from taking meds such as nitrazepam for the nightmares or valium for the anxiety their future will hold. It's my responsibility to ensure these ladies know exactly what will become of them should they take that job.

Suddenly, out of the blue, I heard my name being called from a bullhorn, "Penny, Penny, over here!" And there she was, Paula, as I lived and breathed, in her skirt, on the lunch table. Boy, was it good to see her! I ran over to her, and the two of us hugged like we were best friends and hadn't seen each other for years. I even had tears in my eyes. I said, "Wait, where are the other ladies?"

Well, Cher left to go to another school as an HR assistant full-time. Sure, she did, I was thinking. She flew back to Wuhan. But I'll never let Paula know I knew the truth the entire time. She's better off not knowing. I wished I didn't.

And the other girls are out in the field. They'll be breaking soon enough. Just then, out of the corner of my eye were purple paws rummaging through the garbage. Breakfast was over. I spotted those gawd damn sugar waffles! I then saw Paula looking over as well. We both caught our eyes, smiled, and winked. Bad habits are hard to break.

I met the new principal, Mr. Ollie. What a lovely man. He was perfect for elementary school. He dressed all colorful. I don't know how else to say it. Like crayons. He was no Doc Robert with his tailored ensemble, all bougie and shit; no, Mr. Ollie was his own guy. He almost looks like he would stand outside his office and hand out Rainbow Whirley lollipops to the kids who came to see him. His voice was perfect for the character as well. Just a genuinely lovely guy who immediately allowed me to feel welcome. I'm humbled to be in his presence. What a change from Armpit.

My 3.5-hour day went by extremely fast. And what a great day it was. I left the school grounds and remembered the walk and the ride home like yesterday. Some of the employees have left the school. It has changed in some ways. But that is a constant change. I thought it strange that I didn't even think about Connor until now. I thought I would be thinking about him the entire day.

Maybe emotional pain does get better as time passes. Connor will permanently be etched on my heart, but I must move past this and continue with my life. God has a special place for his angel. I need to leave him alone. I promised to do so.

When my husband came home, I told him about my wonderful day. I assured him that I had given Connor to God and would no longer ruin our lives over his loss and that we needed to move on and start a family of our own. My husband's beautiful blue eyes were so bright and blue, just like the day of our wedding. We made passionate love that night and fell asleep in each other's arms.

The following day was business as usual. It was scorching, and I was finished with this fecking gawd damn baseball field watching these kinders as soon as I arrived. Ever since Cher left, guess who fell into her Chinese slippers? And now I've developed this paranoia regarding balls flying in the air. It didn't matter whether it was a tether ball, basketball, football, or tennis ball; I was afraid of them all. I get moody in the sun.

Most importantly, it's not good for my complexion, even if I carry an umbrella. And if that weren't enough to set "the ball rolling," the damn water fountain was broken again. How could this even be possible that on the hottest days, the water fountain breaks? It's uncanny. I must talk to the union about this. I think they get a kick out of me anyway. I contact them a lot. Keep them in the loop about what's going on around here. I mean, they have a job to do. And that's making sure we are happy. So on my list of to-dos, I will call Katie at the union, water fountain breaks in Death Valley.

It's almost Christmas time, and I'm chipper as can be. Who cares about making money if you're happy at what you do for a living? Besides, not many people I've met can honestly say they love what they do for a living. It's usually about financial gain. But since I don't have to worry about that, remember trust fund baby, I can do this… for now.

My favorite thing I used to love was walking around Manhattan at Christmas time and just window shop. It's funny how Manhattan is such a big city at 13.4 miles long. One block could be dedicated to the rich and famous, and the next block over, you'd better have eyes on the back of your head. I also like to see how many miles I've walked on my Apple Watch. If I knew how to use the damn thing, it would be worth something to me, but technical, you might as well be speaking Mandarin to me. That's as far as it goes. Who cares I just bought myself the Dyson Airwrap! Now I can look like I'm just coming from the beach if I want. These are the things that matter. Not how to play around with an Apple Watch.

I often wondered if the phonies just pretend they know how to work the watch, like read the texts and emails like they're so popular and all the while it's just ads because they haven't a clue either. Oh, that makes me laugh. Just like Façade Book. How can one person has "1.3k" followers? Really? I remember you back in high school, and you had three friends. Now you're so *popular*! Awe c'mon, phony. How many did you actually stalk and whose picture did you use? And how did you get such a perfect life with that perfect husband and the perfect children with the perfect home and the perfect pictures? It's a gawd damn façade. Who are you kidding? You look like a jackass if you didn't want to know the truth. I am veracious, truthful, and veridical! The excitement in the air and all the decorations thrilled me. Bundling up the first snowstorm, wrapping gifts, and finding the right bow. Somehow a California Christmas isn't as exciting for me. But be that as it may, today, I feel spirited and inspired.

I won't let the fact that the last invitro didn't work. That makes three in a row. I won't go through it again. I trust in God that he has my best interests in mind. It's still so sad and disappointing.

It's not the money. It's the excitement that it may just work this time. How could it fail again? We decided to take a break from hormones, in vitro, fertility tests, and pregnancy tests and enjoy each other for a while. The pressure, anxiety, and disappointment are more than "any man" can handle.

I'm walking in a dreamy state and not paying attention to all the security vans, news teams, and my principal, Mr. Ollie. All of them were in front of the school, blocking my entrance. I looked around and spotted Purple Paws. I mouthed to her, "What's going on?"

She whispered, "Wait," and smiled a great wide smile. I took note that she had the Cadillac version of dentures.

WBCN: Mr. Olli, how does it feel to have your student back in your school almost one and one-half years later?

Mr. Ollie: I must admit, I am a very proud colleague of the Newport Elementary School and am so happy Connor O'Leary is back with us. I know the students and teachers missed him terribly. But in all fairness, Dr. John Roberts initially spearheaded this school to help find Connor.

WBCN: Well, where is Dr. Roberts now?

Let's have a word with him.

I'm sorry, but that won't be possible. Mr. Roberts has taken a hiatus and moved to Texas. I'm sure he will see the story later.

I'm so shocked that I don't notice the tears streaming down my face. The mascara was all over my white shirt. I can hardly breathe.

Pretty soon, just like Jesus and his disciples saw Lazarus, I'm going to see Connor! This is really happening. I know a lot of people in a circle surrounding somebody. That has got to be Connor. I don't want him to see me like this. I'll go to the unisex bathroom to freshen up. I'm just hoping that somebody doesn't walk in. I am crying, and I cannot stop. I thanked God as often as I pleaded for him to get Connor home safely.

So here goes. I excused myself through the crowd, my stomach feeling like it was being gutted. I don't even know what to say or how to say it; am I able to hug Connor? Is that even allowed? Is he emotionally damaged that it may be a trigger? I don't want anything to go wrong. I've waited for this day for a long, long time. God, please just give me the right words or the right actions.

Suddenly, I felt the lollipop in my coat pocket. It was a miracle. I walked up to Connor; he looked up at me with his sad, big blue eyes, and I handed him the lollipop. It was melted, and the wrapper was quite crinkled, but I managed to say, "I kept this for you until I saw you again." My eyes watered, and he handed his mom the lollipop. With that, he lunged into my arms and gave me the hugest hug that no Gummy Bear song could ever compare. As I walked away, I heard a voice shout, "Hey, can I go to the bathroom?"

We were on the road before Safe Ship Movers put our last belongings box onto the twenty-six-foot moving truck. It wasn't too bad moving in September. In fact, it was pretty nice. We decided a few months back that there were more reasons to leave California than to stay.

It was hard to say goodbye to the girls I considered family for so long. But things had changed. We all took separate paths eventually, and soon, Connor would be going to school across the way. So we set off for the deep south with a veritable cavalry of interesting and just plain odd characters and odd experiences in my rearview mirror. And a new venture begins.

About the Author

Stephanie Neal received her Bachelor of Administration degree at Adelphi University, New York. After many years working in Manhattan, she moved to the beach communities of Southern California and pursued her degree in Early Childhood Education. She met her husband, Dr. Neal, in 2015, and they are happily married. They spend much time with their dog, Oliver, who agrees to tolerate them in his house. They both enjoy travel, live music, surfing, and fine dining.

Her interests include classic literature, and she has a macabre interest in horror movies.

Recently, they've chosen to move to beautiful South Carolina, and a new adventure begins…

Printed in the USA
CPSIA information can be obtained
at www.ICGtesting.com
LVHW042342071224
798390LV00002B/334